METACOGNITIVE APPROACHES TO ENGLISH LANGUAGE ACQUISITION

DR VEENA JOSEPH

Thank God Almighty, Lord Jesus Christ and Holy Spirit for their constant guidance, grace and blessings on my research.

Contents

Foreword *vii*

Acknowledgements *ix*

1. Introduction 1

2. Role Of The Educator In The Teaching And Learning Process 24

3. Critical Thinking In English Language Acquisition 46

4. Metacognitive Strategies In English Language Acquisition 70

Conclusion 85

Foreword

This book is a must for all academicians striving for excellence in teaching learning pedagogy.
Dr John Joseph

Acknowledgements

The unstinting support of my husband Rev. Dr. John Joseph who has been a pillar of strength and incredible help in completing my book.

My wonderful children Rachel and her husband Andrew, my grandson Ezekial Liam Soans, and Sarah who tirelessly helped, supported, encouraged and stood alongside of me in my entire study. I would acknowledge the love and strong support of my mother and my brothers and sisters.

I would always remain grateful for God's guidance and the leading of the Holy Spirit.

CHAPTER I

INTRODUCTION

In every country that is plugged into the Global economy, there is a call for youths to acquire English proficiency to participate in local and transnational activities, although literacy skills are important, the acquisition of spacer English competencies for Global communication has become an imperative. No longer can language learning rely solely on the printed word, focusing only on improving their reading and writing skills, but also proficiency in listening and speaking in English has become more important than ever. One enables for an individual's personal and professional success in our globalized world where English is the language for international communication, proficient listening and speaking skills also contribute to the academic success of language learners.

The impact of globalization has propelled the teaching of English with greater urgency and has major implications for the language teaching contexts in which English is prioritized above other immediate educational concerns and over the promotion of bi / multilingualism.

It may not be out of place to say that English is no longer just our window to the world, or the link language, or any other tool of restricted use as it was in the past. It has now become the language of our daily life, and there is hardly a domain where English is not used.

In India, where English is not the medium of instruction at some university, it is necessary to adopt special methods to secure an adequate knowledge of English as a second language. One has, after all, only

limited time and energy to invest in English language learning and it is difficult to decide upon the priorities, such as to what extent it should be learnt? In a multilingual and multidialectal context, as in India, these questions are no longer only academic; as it is difficult to think of success in any career in India without adequate proficiency in English.

Today, it is difficult to think of success in any career in India without adequate proficiency in English. That even when a change in the medium of instruction is made, English should continue to be studied by all University students.

On the whole, it may not be out of place to say that English is no longer just our window to the world, or the link language, or any other tool of restricted use as it was in the past. It has now become the language of our daily life, and there is hardly a domain where English is not used.

In India, English is taught along with other languages. One has, after all, only limited time and energy to invest in learning English language and it is difficult to decide upon the priorities. Students and teachers have to facilitate their goals and aspirations for English Language Learning. In a multilingual and multidialectal context, as in India, the thrust for English Language Learning is no longer only academic, they concern the teacher on a day to day basis. learners may identify themselves with time, age, education, job, habits, Lifestyles & the cultural Values they have. This allows for greater learner autonomy and the learner's control of his/her own learning. It permits varying trends of learning among a group of learners and makes language learning an individual activity. This would contribute to high learner motivation and make learning relevant to individual needs and perceptions.

1. Language Acquisition:

Language learning takes place through a process of habit formation; good habits are reinforced by repetition and reward. Making patterns of vocabulary and sentence structure a part of the habit system should be the main goal of language acquisition.

Chomsky says "that the actual language performance of the speaker or hearer is a complex matter that involves many factors... performance, that is what the speaker-hearer actually does, is based not only on knowledge of the language, but on many other factors as well- factors such as memory restrictions, inattention, distraction, non-linguistic knowledge, beliefs and so on" (Chomsky 1968:3)

Nida (1956) and Spolsky (1969), feel that the learner's attitude to a language affects the nature and intensity of his motivation to learn and be a cultural factor. In a typical language learning situation there are a number of people whose attitudes to each other can be significant: the learner, the teacher, the learner's peers, parents, and speakers of the language. Each relationship might well be shown to be a factor controlling the learner's motivation to acquire language, thus, may vary from community to community and individual to individual. An individual verbal item is likely to resemble that of any other(s) only to the extent of the individual's motivation.

Student's motivation to learn a language is thought to be determined both by his attitudes and by the type of orientation one has toward learning that language.

There are many learners of English in India with adequate and comprehensible input, language learning proceeds to hearing and speaking, reading and writing. In India especially with regard to English, learners begin with writing and reading come to speech only towards the end of their learning very little curriculum time is given to teaching oral skills. It is therefore not unusual to find a large number of English users who are fairly proficient in reading and writing, but cannot speak well. The confusion in the order of learning also seems responsible to a certain extent, for errors in the performance of English users. In case of English language learning, that is not always the case, For most learners of English in India their teachers are the only models of language use. Their teachers are likely to have learnt English in the classroom and from books and may not be very fluent speakers themselves. English learners at school or college are exposed to English, not only in the English classroom but also in the subject classes.

Even if we assume that the English teacher is a good model, we cannot be sure that the use of English by subject teachers is satisfactory. Many problems attribute to their models. Mother tongue phonology cannot be held responsible for many errors of pronunciation that we observe around us, prepositions and a few other elements, attitude and motivation in English language learning. It is extremely important to have a positive attitude and motivation to be successful, especially in English language acquisition.

The importance of the emotional factor is easily seen if we consider affective aspects of the learner. The cognitive theory tells us that learners will learn when they actively think about what they are learning. This cognitive factor presupposes the affective factor of motivation.

Listening, reading are fundamental skills for independent language learning in particular for learner of English. The advances in technology provide opportunities to access English, but teaching learning has struggled to change from traditional methods to methods that endow students with effective way to make use of resources outside the classroom.

The responsibility that independent learners assume involve determining the objectives, defining the contents, progression, selecting methods and techniques to be used, monitoring the procedure of acquisition and evaluating what has been acquired to autonomous learners are purposeful, strategic and persistent in their learning. They are self-initiators that is they generate and direct their own learning experience, in addition independent learners are likely to have more adaptive cognition motivation (Chunk & Zimmerman, 1994)

The second is monitoring progress which involves checking on learning and assessing the knowledge learnt. The ability to evaluate one's own progress in accordance with the set goals and to revive subsequent behaviour is essential. To promote learning autonomy two sets of variables are involved i.e. learning and environment. In first of these the learner variable involves existing knowledge, motivation and metacognitive engagement, Littlewood (1996) also suggest that instructors should consider students motivation, confidence and a systematic approach to familiarizing students with the range of learning variable e.g. existing knowledge and skills relevant to learning autonomy and to increase their ability and willingness to engage in independent learning. He suggests that these components go hand in hand developing strategies for autonomy. Therefore, the interaction between metacognitive knowledge and the regulation of that knowledge enhance motivation and vice versa. Based on this interaction, independent learning is possible if learners have a strong capacity to transfer acquired knowledge to new situation either in the same subject area or other field.

If you are an English Language learner for eg – taking a certain Course, when asking you about the impact of visual auditory tools on your learning process and which is more effective for you, you might not be able to answer that, because your cognitive skills allows you to learn, reason and perceive what the usual and auditory (Video / Voice) tools. Metacognition enables understanding, analysis, and control of one's Cognitive processes. It is also known as active learning.

Successful high-end metacognitive engagement occurs with the retention of relevant messages / knowledge and this enhances the possibility of transfer of learning across content domains (Dole & Sinatra (1998) Georghiades (2000) agrees that independent learning is possible if learners have a strong capacity to transfer their acquired knowledge to new situations, in the same subject area across field.

Overall, experts stress the importance of learner variables. Therefore, there is considerable consensus in the literature that enhancement of the transfer of learning acquired in college academics to other context within and across disciplines and to wider social contexts can be achieved by encouraging the learners sense of responsibility, however investigating learner's understanding, use of strategies and providing opportunities to prove the success of those strategies takes time.

Language is primarily speech. All structures and vocabulary items are first practiced orally by learners, before moving on to reading and writing. The order advocated for the learning of language skill is: Listening, Speaking, Reading and Writing.

Language is a set of habits, practice forms an essential part of language teaching/ learning context. If the language item is presented in a meaningful situation, the learner can deduce its meaning and context from the situation, and the mother tongue need not be used.

The thrust is on how to equip the learner not only with the lexical and grammatical repertoire of his/her sphere of language use but the strategic ability to communicate effectively in new situations that might arise at work. The humanistic approach tend to see language learning as a process which engages the whole person and not just the intellect. It takes into account the emotional and spiritual needs of the individuals too.

Language cannot be effectively learnt just by informing or telling the learner the right way of doing things, it can be learnt only if learners are made to do things by themselves. Learners would be willing to do things on their own only if there is a genuine involvement on their part. Such total involvement on the part of learners can be guaranteed only if he/she is motivated and interested in the activity.

Instead of being told what to do, the learners are directed to use their own abilities to arrive at their own opinions, draw their own inferences and conclusions about matters which interest them or which they would find naturally relevant in the process of mulling ones problems and performing activities learners use for language. Language is best acquired when it is used for the purpose of communication for producing meanings and when it centers around the learner as an individual.

More recently we have realized that in actual language use, language skills never occur in isolation. We read and write on the basis of what we have read, we listen and write down notes in our notebook, we read books in libraries and talk about them, consequently, we do not have just the written skill but a little bit of reading, combined or integrated with writing or listening which lead to speaking.

English Language Acquisition is about succeeding in attaining material and affective returns that they desire for themselves and it is also about being considered by others as worthy social beings. In both cases learners are engaged in changing their worlds and thus English Language Acquisition is always transformative.

English Language Acquisition involves situations where members of a language must learn the majority language for reasons over which they have little choice and which are typically associated to larger scale world events such as immigration, economic hardship ,occupation, family, school, workplace, media and so on.

Much goes into the definition of what must develop when English Language Acquisition develops, if the insights from the social turn are needed. As Norton (2006) put it second language learners need to struggle to appropriate the voices of others, they need to learn to command the attention of their listeners; they need to negotiate language as practice; and they need to understand the practices of the communities with which they interact.

Further there are three important task factors for vocabulary acquisition these factors are need, search and evaluation. Need refers to whether or not knowledge of a word is necessary for completion of the task. Need is moderate when it is imposed by the task, and strong when it is imposed by the learners. Search is the cognitive aspect of trying to find or figures out the meaning of the new word.

Doing extensive reading takes up valuable class time, so there are suggestions to try to engage English Language learners in exposures outside the classroom as much as possible. Thus, linking in class activities helps maximize benefits for vocabulary acquisition; Summer Internship Programmes are one such Practical Solutions.

Vocabulary learning from extensive reading and exposure to English language acquisition can be beneficial particularly for advanced learners. Therefore learners should be provided with numerous ways of engaging with the English language acquisition with motivation and fun linking in class activities with out of class activities helps maximize benefits for vocabulary acquisition with technological advances,

Views on English Language Learning:

There are three currently popular views of language, namely: Cognitive, Behavioral and Social. All of these views also have implications for the theory of language learning. It will help us understand the dynamics of language learning and the mechanics of good pedagogy.

1. Cognitive View:

Cognitive view suggests that the different processes concerning can be explained by analyzing the mental process. The functioning of the thought process during learning is influenced by both intrinsic and extrinsic factors.

Cognition includes a wide range of mental processes if it must operate every time we acquire some information, place it in storage, transform that information, and use it. For example the behaviorist approach emphasizes observable behaviors and the psychodynamic approach focuses on unconscious emotions.

1. Cognition involves the active processing of information.
2. Cognition depends greatly upon previous experience (top-down processing).
3. Human cognitive processing abilities are limited.
4. Cognition involves selective and, often, incomplete processing.
5. Cognition often involves parallel processing.

2. Behavioral View:

Behavioral psychologists suggested that language learning was learning a set of habits reinforced by rewards and discouraged by 'punishment'. The thrust is on how to equip the learner, not only with the lexical and grammatical repertoire of his/her sphere of language use, but the strategic ability to communicate effectively in new situations that might arise at work, that is, not merely the surface features but the 'underlying competence' required to negotiate what Hutchison and Waters refer to as 'Target Performance Repertoire'. Though not exclusive learning, the communicative approach has contributed to broadening the perspective learning.

The behaviorist's emphasis on observable behavior led them to reject terms referring to mental events such as image, idea or thought. Many behaviorists classified thinking as simply sub vocal speech.

Presumably appropriate equipment could detect the tiny movements made by the tongue (observable behaviors) during thinking. For ex. If you are thinking while reading this sentence some early behaviorists would have said that you are really just talking to yourself, but so quietly that your vocalizations cannot be heard. Behaviorists also valued experimental control. An important development in Europe at the beginning of the twentieth century was Gestalt psychology (pronounced "Geh-shtablt") Gestalt psychology emphasizes that" humans have basic tendencies to organize what they see and that the whole is greater than the sum of its parts. "

3. Social View:

Sociolinguistics or the study of language in its social setting began to develop in the sixties. The development of sociolinguistics shifted the emphasis from an abstract study of the rules of language to concrete acts of language use.

Many sociologists consider language to be a form of social behavior. Language, according to them, has relevance only in a social context. It can neither be learnt nor used outside a social context. Change in any aspect of this context results in a change in structure and use of language by individuals. So the best way of looking at language may be to look at it as a social phenomenon.

The study of the teaching and learning of any language has to be made keeping in view the fact that language is a social phenomenon. Language is not only an abstract system of formal, lexical and grammatical features but also fulfils a social function and has to be viewed against the social context of its use.

4. Humanistic View:

The humanistic approach tends to see language learning as a process which engages the whole person and not just the intellect. It takes into account the emotional and spiritual needs of the individuals too.

Metacognition:

Defining Metacognition:

English Language learning requires the learners to fully understand the adequate usage and formation of the language. In a fast paced world, language learning cannot be restricted to classroom teaching, but requires the learner's to develop the capacity to learn by themselves, this needs to involve the learner's willingness and ability to take responsibility for their learning. This can be initiated by introducing "Metacognitive process" in teaching and learning of the language

Metacognitive skill is thinking about 'The techniques one can apply' to learn language, not just applying them. Beyond the technique, your mind can think of developing further techniques to make learning easier.

Meta is a prefix from Greek meaning beyond or behind. "Cognition" refers to the mental result of perception, learning, and reasoning. The whole term means what lies behind the ways of thinking that result in perception and reasoning. It is like thinking of the ways of thinking. The process of reasoning while learning is a cognitive skill that depends on logical reasoning and learning thereafter.

Metacognition enables to become successful learners and has been associated with intelligence. The Merriam Webster dictionary defines it as "awareness or analysis of one's own learning or thinking processes in other words metacognition is the knowledge that a person has of his/ her own cognitive processes.

These aspects are crucial to metacognition. The first is self- awareness. The first stage to effective learning is to know one's learning style that is whether the learning is visual, auditory or kinesthetic where a learner knows their individual learning style, they can take measure which will enable them to process the information more efficiently.

Language acquisition is a complex process that involves both knowing information and knowing how to utilize it. Students have to be made aware of the fact that by merely attending classes, they are not going to learn the language. They have to be actively involved in the learning strategy so as to learn the language they have to be engaged in all the activities.

Maintaining motivation to complete a task is also a metacognitive skill together with the ability to become aware of and resist to distracting stimuli in order to sustain effort over time – this is known as cognitive control. Too often teachers teach students what to think but not how to think, what to learn but not how to learn. Learning, how to learn relies basically, on thinking how to think. Thinking how to think, in other words, metacognition occurs in situation when learners become aware of the fact that their cognition, their capacity to understand something has failed them (for example, not being able to understand content or relation e.g. grammar rules) and therefore, they have to work in order to make sense of it. Thus, the metacognitive act includes two elements or stages the learner realizes that there are limitation to everybody's knowledge to complete a task.

Concept of Metacognition:

We cannot say, as even today, we know relatively little about 'language' or language acquisition/ learning', or about the mind/brain which is assumed to have a vital role in this process. About the mind or brain, as Chomsky admits (1986: 39), "we know very little". We know little also about the mental processes involved in learning a language.

The center of these cognitive functions in the brain is the prefrontal cortex located directly behind the forehead. Goldberg describes the prefrontal cortex as the brain's "Chief Executive Officer" for its role in forming goals and objectives and then in devising plans of action required to obtain these goals. It selects the cognitive skills required to complete the plans coordinates these skills and applies them in correct order (2009, P 23). More recent research (Fleming 2014) also identifies this area of the brain specifically the anterior prefrontal Cortex as the center of metacognition.

Cognitive as well as Metacognitive skills could be developed in early childhood. It results in the ability of understanding and analyzing one's own learning methods. Developing metacognitive skills is an ongoing process. If learners are not used to it and you ask them for example to "monitor and assess their own progress in learning" they won't be able to do so unless trained to think beyond the thinking they do to learn or acquire.

In addition to teaching cognition skills, it is important that language teachers support students in building metacognition skills. One of the most important mission of educators is to teach students how to learn on their own throughout their lifetime. How we learn, how to learn, how we know what we have learned and how to direct our own future learning are all questions addressed by the concept of metacognition.

If cognition involves perceiving, understanding, remembering then metacognition involves thinking about one's own perceiving understanding and remembering.

Role of Metacognition:

Metacognition thus refers to an awareness of and reflections about one's knowledge, experiences, emotions and learning in the contexts of language learning and teaching. Cognition can be applied to other disciplines, such as education, communication, business, clinical psychology, social psychology, medicine, and law and consumer psychology.

Cognition refers to how information is processed and learned by the human mind (the term comes from the Latin Verb Cognoscere; to get to know). We are far from a satisfactory understanding of English Language form of cognition. This is because our capacities to investigate the relevant questions are shaped by the pace at which new theories and methods to inspect the workings of human minds and brains become available and the role at which English Language Acquisition becomes conversant in them.

Several key assumption made by information processing psychologists have been in current English language Acquisition about cognition. First the human cognitive architecture is made of representation and access, second mental processing is dual, comprised of two different kinds of computation; automatic or fluent (unconscious) and voluntary or controlled (conscious).

Another cognitive resources such as attention and memory are limited. Two types of memory are crucial in all cognitive operation long term memory and working memory both are fundamentally involved in English Language processing and learning.

As much knowledge or probably more is encoded in implicit procedural memory these are things that we know, without knowing that we know, without knowing that we know, the implicit procedural memory supports skills and habit learning and it is served by the neo cortex in the human brain. Together with memory attention is another essential component of cognition. One main characteristics of attention is that its capacity is limited. Only one attention demanding processing task can be handled at the same time.

Association of Language Awareness (ALA) defines language awareness as “explicit knowledge about language, and conscious perception and sensitivity in language learning, language teaching and language use”. Consequently, the sub ordinate category, Metacognition, relates to an awareness of and reflection on one’s knowledge, experiences, emotions and learning in all domains, whereas its subordinate category, Language awareness, relates to reflections on one’s knowledge, experiences, emotions and learning in three sub domains: Language, Language learning and Language teaching.

Metacognition in Learning:

Metacognition enables understanding, analysis, and control of one’s Cognitive processes. It is also known as active learning. It helps the learner, not only to learn, reason and perceive what the process offers, but enables them to decide which learning process is effective.

This allows for greater learner autonomy and the learner’s control of his/her own learning. It permits varying levels of learning among a group of learners and makes language learning an individual activity. This would contribute to high learner motivation and make learning relevant to individual needs and perceptions.

Instead of being told what to do, the learners are directed to use their cognitive abilities to arrive at their own opinions, draw their own inferences and conclusions about matters which would interest them or which they would find naturally relevant. And in the process of mulling over problems and performing activities learners use language (structures, functions, words and skills). The assumption is that language is best acquired when it is used for the purpose of communication for producing meanings, and when it centers around the learner as an individual.

In actual language use, language skills never occur in isolation. We listen while we speak, we read and write on the basis of what we have read, we listen and write down notes in our notebook, and we read books in libraries and talk about them and so on.

Consequently, we do not have just the written skill but a little bit of reading, combined or integrated with writing or listening which leads to speaking. These are the more obvious combinations – reading and writing, listening and speaking. There are also other skills integrated quite meaningfully – listening with writing, speaking with writing, and so on.

One other very important feature of learner-centered materials is the ways they make the learners deploy their cognitive abilities/thinking skills. Since these materials also believe that language skills involve cognitive sub-skills, they make the learners predict, anticipate, guess from the context, and use their previous experience.

In addition to self-reflection regarding knowledge and beliefs, it is critical that teachers know how they can create a learning environment where students can be involved in metacognition, i.e. to reflect on and explore their knowledge and beliefs about languages and cultures, abilities and learning.

Self-assessment is a useful method for learners to develop metacognitive skills, as they learn to recognize their own abilities and deficits. Metacognitive skills are generally divided into "self-assessment (the ability to assess one's own cognition) and self-management (the ability to manage one's further cognitive development)" (Ibabe and Jauregizar 2010, 246). Hence, students who are able to accurately self- assess their skills are more likely to develop strategies for their learning process and therefore perform better than those who are unaware of their strengths and shortcomings.

However, in most classrooms, very few teachers report giving their learners the opportunity to try out various learning strategies for themselves, reflect on their learning with others, set goals for their own learning, and, ultimately, evaluate their own performance. Thus, the key elements of metacognition instruction—that is, letting learners be active in exploring and reflecting on their own knowledge and learning—seem to be missing in language learning classes.

Certain principles are part of most metacognitive instructional models: the activation of learners' prior knowledge, reflections on what learners know and want to learn, explanations and modeling of learner strategies by the teacher, and learners' own involvement in making goals for monitoring and evaluating the learning process. For example, Anderson (2002, 2008) suggests that metacognition about learning consists of five primary components or skills which can be trained in the language classroom. For all components, the teacher has a key role in explaining, modeling and creating an atmosphere which encourages reflective discourse. The following components are suggested by Anderson:

1. **Preparingand planning for learning.** Students reflect on what they need or want to accomplish and what they can do to accomplish their learning goals.
2. **Selecting and using learning strategies.** Anderson (2002, 3) states that "the metacognitive ability to select and use particular strategies in a given context for a specific purpose means that the learner can think and make conscious decisions about the learning process".
3. **Monitoring strategy use.** Students should be trained to keep track of their strategy use. While in a learning process, students could, for example, ask themselves questions about their strategy choices, how well particular Metacognitive strategies work, and to what extent they use them the way they intended.
4. **Orchestrating various strategies.** For most learning tasks, students must apply several strategies. Thus, it is beneficial to students in their learning process to effectively coordinate the various strategies they know.
5. **Evaluating strategy use and learning.** The fifth component is summed up in four questions that Anderson suggests should be asked cyclically during the learning process:

1. What am I trying to accomplish?
2. What strategies am I using?
3. How well am I using them?
4. What else could I do?

Anderson emphasizes that these questions can be regarded as the essence of the first four components and that all of them work best together.

Metacognitive approaches to English language acquisition has been proposed to develop learners who can communicate fluently but also accurately. One approach to English language Acquisition that has been proposed to develop learners who can communicate fluently but also accurately is focus of form, interest in focus on form has grown since its original inception, and today is considered a leading paradigm for English language Acquisition, on the interface between theory and practice.

Metacognition in Teaching:

Metacognitively aware teachers reflect on their knowledge, beliefs and teaching practices; they plan, implement, monitor and evaluate their own teaching as well as students' learning on a daily basis and use their insights to improve teaching. Regarding language teachers, they should ideally have a reflective approach to their work in at least four different ways (see Svalberg 2007 for a related discussion, and Hiver and Whitehead 2018, this volume), namely as:

1. English Language users: English Language teachers should be proficient in English language and know how to serve as language models for their learners.

2. Culture educators: Teachers have a key role in promoting learners intercultural competence. For this reason, they need to have knowledge of intercultural communication as well as how they can help learners adjust their own thinking and behaviour. In interaction with other 22 Åsta Haukås people Dypedahl (2018, this volume) explores some general principles for designing courses in language teacher education that can enhance such a metacognitive approach to intercultural learning. He suggests that intercultural awareness should be regarded as one integral component of intercultural

competence, defining it as the conscious monitoring and adjustment of one's own thinking and interaction with other people. Among other things, this involves "a conscious understanding of the role culturally based forms, practices, and frames of understanding can have in intercultural communication, and an ability to put these conceptions into practice in a flexible and context specific manner in real time communication" (Baker 2012, 66). Furthermore, teachers should reflect on how they can assist their learners in the process of becoming more aware of culturally based norms, beliefs and behaviors. This should be combined with broad cultural knowledge of the teacher's own country and the countries where the target language is spoken.

3. Language Teachers: Language teachers must have knowledge of how languages are learned and how they can help learners enhance their own learning by assigning an active role to the learners. Language teachers should motivate their learners to reflect on what they know about language(s), culture(s) and language learning and how they can develop their knowledge further.

Metacognition in English Language Acquisition:

Henry Sweet divided the learning of the target language into four stages: (Kudchedkar: 2002):

<u>Mechanical</u>

Pronunciation of words and sentences is mastered thoroughly.

<u>Grammatical</u>

The grammatical categories in the text are identified and taught. The teaching of grammar is graded from easy to difficult.

<u>Idiomatic and Lexical</u>

Idioms and new vocabulary in the text and other sources
are taught systematically.

<u>Literary</u>

Graded texts from contemporary literature are studied.

The ultimate aim of the direct method was to develop in the learners, the ability to think in the language, whether in speaking, reading or writing.

- The process of learning is essentially one of forming associations: speech with appropriate action, words with concepts and objects. The associations have to be direct, concrete and definite, and cross-associations which conflict with each other have to be avoided.

- Repetition is essential if associations have to be formed and reinforced. The teacher should begin with a limited number of items.
- Memory depends not only on repetition, but attention and interest as well. So if a learner is motivated and wants to learn a language she/he will do it.
- The teaching materials, namely texts, dictionaries and grammar should be interrelated and coordinated to make learning effective.

Two types of reading were introduced - extensive and intensive. Extensive reading was done by the learner on his/her own, whereas intensive reading texts were used a base for grammar study, vocabulary acquisition and reading sentences for comprehension. Translation was discouraged, and learners were encouraged to infer the meaning from the context, or from cognates in his/her own language.

For English Language Teaching in India today, however, West's work appears to have three lessons which we could like to draw in three brief statements. First, that good English Language Teaching must risk theory to be judged in the ordinary classroom. Secondly, that curriculum renewal is a problem in education as whole and not just language education and it therefore has to be based on neutral studies of the educational system in all its essentials. And lastly, that the four areas west singled out for deep study and analysis, namely, Indian multilingualism, reading and its teaching, vocabulary study and word teaching and materials design and development, ought to be focused on as much today as they were by him in his day.

It will help the learner to gain access to the reserve powers of the mind. It will bring a harmonious collaboration of the conscious and the unconscious mind. To remove the mental barriers of the learners the following pedagogic principles should be kept in mind:

English language Acquisition enables learners to use language accurately, fluently, and appropriately in meaning – focused contexts. If the desired goal of instruction is the ability to communicate freely in the English language. Rich and plentiful input that engages learners in communication is the optimal pedagogical choice for English language acquisition.

Acquisition occurs subconsciously as the cognitive system is exposed to various patterns because learning is subconscious instruction has little effect on the processes of acquisitions, nonetheless classroom instruction can bring about optimal conditions for the working of these processes. Acquisition Theory Input processing and the Interaction approach.

Metacognition in Multilingual Learning:

There are plenty of instances to show that a multilingual setting may or may not be an asset, but it is certainly no liability. Multilingualism can be turned into an asset for the language learner. Concepts and expressions in one language can be exploited for learning those in another. English Language Teaching in India can utilize multilingualism as a resource. Apart from being used through translation, which has not lost its relevance, the Indian language(s) known by the learner can also be utilized for creating concepts and for enhancing the choice and the motivation of the learner.

People acquire a second language only if they obtain comprehensible input and if their affective filters are low enough to allow the input in. when the filter is down and appropriate comprehensible input is present (and comprehended), acquisition is inevitable.

In the dictionary sense of the word, it may be all right to Say that people 'acquire' the first language L1 and 'learn' the second language ENGLISH LANGUAGE. After all, the circumstances and results of learning these languages are often quite different for many people. There is a considerable body of literature on the differences between first language and second language acquisition. These differences are presumably owing to different circumstances and achievements in acquisition/learning. While everybody has abundant exposure to the language to be learnt in the context of First Language Acquisition (FLA), it is not always so with the second language. Neither does everyone get to learn the second language in 'natural' circumstances like one's first language. People often learn it through instruction.

Attempting to distinguish between the first language acquisition and second language learning, Krashen says: "There are two independent ways to developing ability in second languages. Acquisition is a subconscious process identical in all important ways to the process children utilize. In acquiring their first language, while learning is a 'conscious' process that results in knowing about language (1985:1)"

Teachers and learners should be clear on their goals in studying an ENGLISH LANGUAGE because these goals should dictate the best types of instruction. In some cases, it is possible for communication in the ENGLISH LANGUAGE to occur outside the classroom in uninstructed ENGLISH LANGUAGE acquisition and indeed some strong versions of communication language teaching propose that interaction inside ever.

It seems now reasonably well-established, that there is a special component of the human brain (call it 'the language faculty'), that is specifically dedicate to language. The language faculty 'grows' from the initial state through childhood, reaching a relatively steady state at some stage of maturation. This is the process of language acquisition, sometimes misleadingly called 'language learning'. The process seems to bear little resemblance to what is called 'learning'.

Hence, the same universal principles govern both first and second language acquisition, although 'there will be interference, differences in processing capacities, general decreasing plasticity, and a failure to keep acquisition abilities active, rather than to any type of language ability shutdown

It has also been found that cognitive processes of learning as by rule-formation, facilitate older learners to acquire language faster than by the natural process of unconscious acquisition. Learning, particularly the learning of a language, is an emotional experience, and the feelings that the learning process evokes, will have a crucial bearing on the feelings for the task is vital for the success of the task.

Metalinguistic awareness, via its close relationship to metacognitive knowledge and awareness of that knowledge, has been studied from an increasing number of research perspectives in the field of multilingual development. Metalinguistic awareness can be described as the ability to both focus on linguistic form and switch focus between form and meaning. Individuals who are linguistically aware will be able to both categorize words into parts of speech and switch their focus between form, function and meaning. They will also be able to explain why a word has a particular function. Consequently, the distinction between explicit and implicit learning is linked to the development of levels of metalinguistic awareness

Multilingual activities can be designed for multilingual classes but also adapted to English language classes in such a way that they can support the development and use of the language. They can also be integrated into subject Metacognition in Multilingual Learning teaching in general and will, as is our claim, contribute to more efficient (language) learning and teaching. Multilingual approaches motivate students to develop more language learning strategies and expand the types of strategies they use.

Thus, metacognitive decision-making in the process of language planning and use on the individual level is influenced by the speakers' perceived needs. The level of multilingual awareness plays a considerable role in all these processes; for instance, when comparing levels of proficiency between the languages of a speaker. Related to the issue of perceived communicative needs is perceived level of proficiency or knowledge in language learners, which plays a vital role in self- assessment.

Metacognitive approaches to English language acquisition have been proposed to develop learners who can communicate fluently but also accurately. One approach to English language Acquisition that has been proposed to develop learners who can communicate fluently but also accurately is focus of form, interest in focus of form has grown since its original inception, and today is considered a leading paradigm for English language Acquisition, on the interface between theory and practice.

Instruction may help learners progress through the stages, allow learners to achieve higher levels of accuracy, than they might have otherwise.

ATTITUDE AND MOTIVATION IN SECONDLANGUAGE LEARNING

It is extremely important to have a positive attitude and motivation for success, especially in second language acquisition. We will look at them in some details now. According to Hutchinson and Waters, 'the importance of the emotional factor is easily seen if we consider the relationship between the cognitive and affective aspects of the learner. The cognitive theory tells us that learners will learn, when they actively think about what they are learning. But this cognitive factor presupposes the affective factor of motivation. Before learners can actively think about something, they must want to think about it. The emotional reaction to the learning experience is the essential foundation for the initiation of the cognitive process. How learning is perceived by the learner will affect what learning, if any, will take place' (Hutchinson and Waters (1987:47)

Attention can be voluntary in the sense that it can be subject to cognitive top down control that is driven by goals and intentions of the individuals. Furthermore, while learning people learn faster and better when they deliberately apply themselves to learning.

Attention is necessary for learning and the central components of attention are alertness, orientation, detection, and noticing is a prerequisite for acquisition. It has been proposed that multiple types of enhancement may lead to deeper cognitive Processing, Furthermore, because theory and research indicate that including attention to language items during meaning-focused interaction is generally more beneficial for English language acquisition than interaction. Learners need multiple encounters with words to achieve long-term retention; however, learners may not experience such recurrent exposure through extensive reading, especially for low frequency words.

Thinking aloud while performing a task is the best window we have into the objects of consciousness both fringe conscious awareness and more qualitative addressing (Baars & Franklins 2003). Debriefing, questionnaires, interview and stimulated recalls, have also been used.

Ellis (2006a) explains that the human architecture of the brain is neurobiologically programmed to be sensitive to the statistical properties of the input and to learn from them. When processing the brain engages in a continuous and mandatory (as well as implicit) in the sense of automatic and certainly unconscious tally of overall frequency of each form and likelihood of co-occurrence with other forms. This statistical tallying is supported by a neural structure in the Neocortex Cell is 2006 (b) probabilistic learning phrases that learning is not categorical but graded and scholastic that it proceeds by (subconscious).

Additional important trend in the emergent list of theories are perhaps broader knowledge are inseparable because we come to know language from using it.

Motivation is often considered by educators as one of the primary reasons, for English language Acquisition, Nonetheless, many researchers and Educators are concerned with how to increase Learner interaction in the classroom. Motivation put simply is the stimulus that drains learners to initiate and sustain English language Acquisition.

Noticing of language features is a first step towards acquisition. Input enhancement can facilitate Learner's noticing of target forms, as well as improve overall comprehension. Additionally, multiple types of enhancement lead to deeper cognitive processing. Including attention to language items during meaning focused interaction.

Interaction is a core construct for communication in the classroom and multiple studies have examined how interactions, and especially negotiation for meaning, occur in the importance of input, interaction, and output. Communication does not happen in a vacuum, learners must talk about something, and provide input for communicative activities allow researchers and teachers to affect task interaction. An important pedagogical outgrowth of the interaction Approach is seen in task-based language learning and teaching which uses a variety of tasks to achieve different types of interaction in the English Language Classroom. In addition to investigating input, negotiation, and output advocates task-based learning, are interested in other variables that affect interaction.

Teachers can raise learner's awareness of the benefits of peer interaction about the benefits of interaction. Teachers can use role plays, games and discussions to encourage learners to interact with each other, teachers can provide instruction on how to recognize learning opportunities during interaction and how to seek and provide communicative assistance. Raising learners awareness takes time and planning, persistent instruction and positive attitudes can hugely benefit students and they will have a feeling of achievement.

The development of communicative competence is much less visible, but if learners are made aware that developing communicative competence through interaction is important, such knowledge may help learners feel that they are indeed learning.

A major variable that has been explored in interaction research is how the structure of meaning-focused activities can result in different types of interaction and affect English language Acquisition, such tasks is considered to be a communicative activity.

Depth of knowledge: - the many aspects of vocabulary knowledge – grammatical function, collocation, frequency, register and domain – all contribute to learners depth of vocabulary knowledge. As a result, learners have the task of not only learning the form meaning, connections of words, but also building up their knowledge of these other components, if learners know only the basic form, meaning connections of lexical items then their depth of knowledge is limited.

Receptive and productive vocabulary knowledge: - Another distinction that is made in vocabulary learning is between productive and receptive knowledge, also referred to as active and passive knowledge respectively (Laufer, 1998; Laufer & Paribakht, 1998; Webb, 2008). Productive knowledge is comprised of words that learners can use when they are creating either written or spoken English Language output. In contrast, receptive knowledge consists of words learners can recognize in the input, but are unable to come up with on their own, Research shows that in general, learners‘ receptive vocabulary knowledge is larger than their productive knowledge.

The breadth of knowledge: - Breadth of knowledge refers to the number of words that learners know, with the knowledge in question consisting simply of the basic form-meaning relationships and not the multiple aspects that comprise the depth of that knowledge. In considering the breadth of vocabulary knowledge there is some discussion about the optimal size of English language speakers' vocabulary. Of course, larger is better, but vocabulary learning takes time, and it is important for learners to have realistic learning goals.

The average adult English LI speaker is conservatively estimated to have a vocabulary size of roughly 20,000-word families (Nation, 2001). For English Language learners, the method often used for calculating a desirable vocabulary size calculate what number of words would allow learners to easily comprehend English Language input. It is assumed that readers need to know about 95%-98% of the words in a text to read easily for comprehension and to be able to make informed guesses about unknown words. By some calculations, this means that learners need to know roughly the 3,000 most frequent words in the English Language (Ntion, 2001; Webb, 2010).

Although the number of times a word is encountered is important, the quality of those encounters is also important. Schmitt (2008) refers to this as engagement, and he advocates that the more engagement learners have, the better it will be retained. Similarly, Laufer and Rozokski-Roitblat suggest that how well words are processed is an essential component of vocabulary acquisition. Finally, Eckert and Tavakoli (2012) draw on the depth of processing hypothesis (e.g. Lockhart & Craik, 1990) to support the element that the intensity of exposure to lexical items is just as important, if not more important, than the frequency of exposure. Shallow processing of a word involving perhaps no more than processing the orthographic or phonological features of a word is less beneficial for vocabulary learning than a deeper analysis, which would include processing the semantic and conceptual characteristics of the word.

Problems in Learning the English Language in India:

Many second or English language learners, such as many learners of English from rural or semi-urban areas in India, have very limited exposure to the language to be learned. They hardly find it used around them at home or elsewhere in their social life.

In India, especially with regard to English, learners begin with writing and reading and come to speech only towards the end of their learning.

Very little curriculum time is given to teaching oral skills. It is therefore not unusual to find a large number of English users, who are fairly proficient in reading and writing but cannot speak well. The confusion in the order of learning also seems responsible to a certain extent, for errors in the performance of second language users.

In the case of second language learning, this is not always the case. For most learners of English in India, their teachers are the only models of language use. These teachers are likely to have learned English in the classroom and from books and may not be very fluent speakers themselves. The average English learner at school or college is exposed to English, not only in the English classroom but also in the subject classes. Even if we assume that the English teacher is a good model, we cannot be sure that the use of English by subject teachers is satisfactory. Many problems are attributed to their models. Mother tongue phonology cannot be held responsible for any errors of pronunciation that we observe around us.

1. Learning takes place best in a relaxed and happy atmosphere.
2. Sufficient listening time should be given for learners to absorb the new material.
3. Active participation helps in the learning of new material.
4. Role play (fantasy) reduces threat and so barriers to learning can be overcome.
5. The functional aspect of language should be emphasized.
6. Fine arts (music, art, drama) aid suggestions and should be integrated with the teaching/learning process.
7. The atmosphere, the material, methods, and techniques should aim at 'infantilization' so that learners have a childlike (open-minded) attitude to learning.

There are, however, other possible ways of learning a language. Some believe that language may not be effectively learned just by informing or telling the learner the right way of doing things; it can be learned only if learners are made to do things by themselves. Learners would be willing to do things on their own only if there is genuine involvement on their part. Such total involvement on the part of the learner can be guaranteed only if he/she is motivated and interested in English Language Acquisition.

CHAPTER II

ROLE OF THE EDUCATOR IN THE TEACHING AND LEARNING PROCESS

Thirty years ago, educators paid little attention to the work of cognitive in classroom learning, scientists, and researchers in the field of cognitive science. Today cognitive researchers are spending more time working with teachers testing and refining their theories in real classroom where they can see how different setting and classroom interactions influence applications of their theories.

In the current scenario, modernization has led to the development in each aspects, including language learning and teaching process. English language is no longer restricted to classrooms, but it is a necessity in excelling in the highly competitive global market.

A very interesting feature of all these learner – centered materials is that they generally seem to believe in a language model too, which is not just structures and words or just communicative functions or skills, but a rich and creative combination of all these in communicative and purposeful use in real life situations, which can be academic, personal, affective, creative and more pragmatic / communicative.

The strategies of learning have drastically advanced and it is further going to evolve dramatically as being for richer than before. One of the hallmarks of the science of learning is its emphasis on learning with understanding.

Teachers aim should be to help students learn and develop their ability to take responsibility for their own learning, and to apply active personal meaningful strategies to their work both inside and outside the classroom, thus helping students to increase their ability to communicate and learn independently. Teachers should also strive to help their students to develop greater autonomy as individuals. They should further enhance confidence, motivation, knowledge and skills that they require in order to communicate more independently, learn more independently and to be more independent as individuals.

Educators role is to drive the brains of students so as to make them self directed learners, by developing their mindset and ability to take charge of their learning in order to take them further in life. Students should start learning about metacognition at an early age and apply it across all content areas in life lessons.

The role of the educator is to communicate knowledge in a clear and structured way, to explain correct solutions, to give students class and resolvable problem, facilitating student's inquiry. Constructionist (Marion Williams, Et al. 1997) held the idea that a teacher's deep-rooted beliefs about how languages are learnt will pervade the classroom actions more than a particular methodology he/ she is told to adopt or the course book he/she follows.

Melodic Rosen field and Sherman Rosen field (2008) claimed from their studies that effective teachers act on the belief that all students can meet the needs of diverse learners and believe that teachers can intervene to make a difference.

Effective teachers have interventionist belief about students: a set of beliefs that inclusive classrooms lead to effective teacher practice, and improved students performance and self-esteem. Effective teachers solve students learning difficulties.

Teachers aim to help students to develop their ability to take responsibility for their own learning and to apply active personally meaningful strategies to their work both inside and outside the classroom. Helping students to increase their ability to communicate and learn independently, language education aim should be to help their students to develop their ability to take responsibility for their own learning and to apply active personally meaningful strategies to their work both inside and outside the classroom.

Helping their students to increase their ability to communicate and learn independently educators should also strive to help their students to develop greater autonomy as individuals. They should further enhance confidence, motivation, knowledge and skills that they require in order to communicate more independently, learn more independently and to be more independent as individuals

The role of metacognition and cognition is particularly critical to English language acquisition, because many mental processes during speech comprehension and production are hidden from teachers and quite often from the learners themselves. Learner's have a vague idea as to their learning strategy, and the problems they might encounter in the process. Teachers therefore need to help students to find ways of understanding and managing their cognitive processes and emotions through activities that raise their metacognitive awareness about listening and speaking.

Education needs to empower students with metacognitive and cognitive skills to achieve success in learning English with their application; students can more constantly achieve their goals to improve both excellence and equity.

Educators can help students to reflect on their individual learning and engage them in metacognitive discussion in the classroom. Educators should celebrate this important skill in large and small groups ways to underscore the many ways this approach comes in handy in the college and other aspects of life, just not students but even their parents can make use of this skill at work. By creating opportunities, the Educators can help release potential of the learner and help them to achieve excellence.

Educators can also increase learner's metacognitive knowledge about feature of the spoken language they have to comprehend and produce as well as develop a repertoire of strategies that enable them to participate effectively. Weak or less proficient students differ from successful ones in many aspects. Among other things weak students often are not aware of their thinking processes and fail to monitor their learning processes. They are in capable of being in charge of their learning.

Successful learners, have a wide variety of thinking skills. They have domain knowledge and are able to apply it to any learning situation. It is an accepted fact that a successful learner possesses metacognition. The conscious ability to recognize their knowledge, understand and have control over their own learning. Students with good metacognition are able to monitor and direct their own learning processes; they have the ability to master information and apply the learning strategies to solve problems more easily. The strategy variables includes knowledge about both cognitive and metacognitive strategies, as well as conditional knowledge about when and where it is appropriate to use such strategies.

Educators can also present a number of examples to illustrate their instruction. Teachers can even model their instruction by using "The Technique" think out loud to show. When and how the metacognitive strategies should be used. Students should be given ample opportunities to perform the same task under the guidance of teachers, in order to internalize them until they become automatic. This application of the strategies serves as independent practice accompanied by teacher's feedback. Recognizing and practice in applying metacognitive strategies will help students successfully in solving problems not only in their subject areas but throughout their lives as well.

English language Acquisition enables learners to use language accurately, fluently, and appropriately in meaning – focused contexts. If the desired goal of instruction is the ability to communicate freely in the English language. Rich and plentiful input that engages learners in communication is the optimal pedagogical choice for English language acquisition.

Educators should be clear on their goals for English language acquisition. Input is essential for English language acquisition. Although researchers agree that input in the form of positive evidence is indispensable for acquisition, they do not all agree on what types of input are best. For one thing, input in and of itself is not particularly useful unit it enters learner's cognitive systems, a process called intake. Thus intake is defined as the part of the input that is noticed, comprehended, and taken in to the cognitive system. There is some consensus that one benefit of classroom instruction is that input can be modified in order to increase the likelihood of its intake.

Research in general suggests that instruction can improve the rate of Acquisition, and instructed learner may program more quickly. Furthermore, instruction may be necessary to achieve higher levels of ultimate attainment and avoid fossilization (Housen & Pierrard, 2005).

Processability theory maintains that the cognitive processing of language occurs relatively automatically and unconsciously. Input is processed in specific ways, with processing at the initial stages of learning limited to small chunks of language and developing to larger units, such as noun phrases and clauses. English language acquisition occurs subconsciously as the cognitive system is exposed to various patterns in the input. English language acquisition occurs subconsciously as the cognitive system is exposed to various patterns in the input learning is subconscious, instruction has little effect on the processes of acquisition, nonetheless, classroom instruction can bring about optimal conditions for the working of these processes. Many researchers, teachers, and learners propose that, in general, the goal of English language Acquisition is to develop communicative competence in learners so that they may use English language for spontaneous communication. English language Acquisition enables learners to communicate effectively for learners should be able to use the language appropriately in various social contexts.

Strategic competence, It has been observed that learners who engaged in interactive tasks, often accompanied by feedback, improved considerable more than learners who did not interact .Educators can raise learners awareness of the benefits of peer interaction.

As a whole educators can use role plays, games, and discussions to encourage learners to interact with each other; educators can also provide instructions on how to recognize learning opportunities, during interaction and how to seek and provide communicative assistance Raising learners awareness takes time and planning, persistent instruction pays off in positive attitudes and interaction behaviors.

Teacher's Role in the Learning Process:

By contrast, Pressley, Borkowski, and Schnvider (1981) highlighted that good readers automatically employ metacognitive strategies to focus their attention, to derive meaning and to make adjustments when something goes wrong.

Educator's role is to drive the brains of students so as to make them self-directed learners, by developing their mindset and ability to take charge of their learning in order to take them further in life. Students should start learning about metacognition at an early age and apply it across all content areas in life lessons.

Educators should look out for innovative ways and methods of teaching and promote active learning like play, drama and making explicit links between out of class knowledge and learning.

Educators need to constantly upgrade their skills for effective teaching is according to the relevant times and use of ICT in teaching and learning. It is extremely imperative that teachers have perception of their technical competence and ability to influence students learning.

The role of the educator is to show ways and strategies that students need to know as to how to go about the learning process. Teachers need to show them how to choose the strategy that has the best chance of success in a given situation.

1. Learning Goals:

Teachers can teach students to set up their learning goals and make plans for learning tasks. By engaging in preparation and planning in relation to a learning goal, students can think about what they need or want to accomplish and how they intend to go about performing it. It is important that teachers should have students be explicit about the particulars learning goals. The clearer the goal is, the easier it will be for students to measure their own progress. For example, in a writing class, students might set a goal for themselves of being able to write a process at the end of a lesson. They may then make such plans as organizing ideas, preparing an outline, and deciding on the techniques to make a paper unified and for example in a writing lesson, students learn several strategies to create a good article, among other things to consider are the "audience" and purpose in writing. Student should be encouraged to constantly question and reason about their task. They have to ever learn to analyze their own skills regarding reading and writing as to even the effectiveness of the said purpose.

2. Thinking Skills:

By encouraging students to evaluate whether or not what they are doing is really effective, teachers can help students to be actively engaged in metacognition.

Teachers have to constantly monitor students and encourage them to respond thoughtfully to the following questions: -

1. What am I trying to accomplish
2. What strategies am I using?
3. How well am I using them?
4. What is the outcome?
5. What else could I do?

Activation of Metacognition:

Metacognition can be taught to students. The approaches in teaching students the metacognitive strategies include direct instruction, teacher modeling, and application. For direct instruction teachers give clear explanation about the strategies to be taught, why they are important and when students will need to use them.

Educator can also present a number of examples to illustrate their instruction. Teachers can even model their instruction by using "The Technique" think out loud to show, when and how the metacognitive strategies should be used. Students should be given ample opportunities to perform the same task under the guidance of teachers, in order to internalize them until they become automatic. This application of the strategies serves as independent practice accompanied by teacher's feedback. Recognizing and practice in applying metacognitive strategies will help students successfully in solving problems not only in their subject areas but throughout their lives as well.

Metacognition is the conscious awareness that one has about his/her knowledge and the conscious ability to monitor and gain control over his/ her own thinking and learning processes.

Metacognition thus is cognitively interwoven with reflection, the active process of exploring events or issues and accompanying thoughts and emotions ()Kerka,2002, p.z). Given that reflection plays an important

role in determining the effectiveness of learning (Daniel 2002) teachers should incorporate into their teaching activities that promote reflective practices along with the development of language pursue. Such activities raise the students awareness of what happens during the English language learning process, thus, leading them to develop their metacognition and learning skills.

Reflective Process:

When students use metacognitive they can take a step back and observe their thinking this is called reflective process. Educator can even encourage students to keep a reflective Journal where in learners can explore ideas, record their thinking processes, feelings and reflections. Journal writing is a vital means of developing metacognition through reflective processes. Teachers can encourage students to write about "what they know" and "what they don't know" as a way to trigger their prior knowledge and "what they want to learn about" to reveal their expectation. Teachers should also have students write about their thoughts, feelings, related experiences beliefs, attitudes in regards to the lesson, "make note of their awareness of ambiguities and in consistencies" (Blakey & Shiela 1990, P2) comment on how they have dealt with difficulties in their learning processes as well as evaluate themselves as learners.

When students use metacognition they can take a step back and observe their thinking this is called reflective process.

Teachers should function as a mental guide, by helping students to focus on the reflective moment rather than as an evaluator correcting or commenting or the students learning process.

Students should be constantly encouraged to use all their four skills respectively in the learning process. Teacher should act as facilitator questions that trigger their metacognition.

It has been accepted that metacognition promotes effective learning in diverse area; students who are skilled in metacognition are more strategic and perform better than those who are less equipped.

Teachers should teach their students metacognitive skills in addition to the language. To do so, teachers can provide direct instruction about how the strategies can be used or take students through each strategy by modeling. Educators must give guided practices, wherein they assume full responsibility for completing a task this entails the strategies of planning, monitoring and evaluating. In addition, metacognition should be taught through classroom activities that foster reflective thinking and practices.

Students should be constantly motivated to learn how things reflect upon their thinking, and evaluate themselves as learners. Such reflection, as Thamraksa (1997) pointed out is important, as it is a means to bring learning to conscious attention, to the level of awareness. Students should also be given ample opportunities to talk out loud about what's on their mind when they engage in a learning task, it is through talking that students come to gain control over their thinking processes. Equally important is the use for self questioning activities in which students ask themselves questions that trigger each stage of their thoughts from planning to approach a particular task monitoring the effectiveness of strategies being applied to the task to evaluating their learning out comes. These activities engage students in a kind of reflection in action of the work they are doing.

Motivation:

Educator needs to upgrade entrance skills of students. Motivate them to improve their memory, which can be by encouraging them to repeat certain things that they need to remember, put it in a chunk, use mnemonics and constantly whenever applicable use it in their conversation.

Encourage students to have an inquisitive mind so as to know the know how of things. Students should be taught to have a mind map; and should focus on a few things only. They should be guided to take things bit by bit.

Educator should be aware of the learners, learning style preferences; the strategies that they like and their language learning aptitude. Teachers also need to think about the attitudes and motivation of learners. Starting with strategies which give them solutions to current learning problems.

Communication skills strategies help students to learn more of the language such as asking for classification, checking for comprehension, paraphrasing and so on. The National Capital Language Resources Centre (NCLRC;2003) has proposed a metacognitive model in which the learners problem – solving goals are at the center of the circular model. Surrounding them learner goals are the metacognitive strategies of planning, monitoring, managing learning, and evaluating language learning and learning strategy effectiveness. Task based learning strategies comprise the outer circle of the model and are grouped into four categories; use what you know. Use your imagination, organizational skills and use a variety of resources. Teacher resources guides developed for elementary immersion classroom (NCLRC,2003) high school foreign and higher education foreign language classroom (NCLRC,2004b) apply this model to classroom instruction.

Teachers can motivate students to do a particular task in a group, a task that provides an outcome and that all can see and comment on.

The teacher's role is of a facilitator, to observe and discuss, monitor progress and efficiency.

The study of English language learning strategies will continue to develop as second language acquisition researchers seek to understand different learner characteristics and the complex cognitive social and affective processes involved in processing language input and using the language for a variety of purpose. Likewise, English language educator and methodologists will continue their quest for more effective instructional approaches and with increasing emphasis on learner. Central instruction and learner empowerment in all areas of education instruction in learning strategies will assume a greater role in teacher preparation and Curriculum design.

The role of the educator is to develop student's ability to operate independently with the learning of English language and use the language to communicate in real, unpredictable situations. Teachers aim is to help students develop their ability to take responsibility for their own learning and to apply active personal meaningful strategies to their work both inside and outside the classroom. Teachers must help their students to increase their ability to communicate and learn independently. Language teachers also try to reach the goal of helping their students to develop greater autonomy as individuals, teachers need to motivate students to gain confidence, knowledge and skills that they require in order to communicate more independently. This methodology will enhance their personality and check out better individuals.

Teachers must learn to focus on the students, as each student is unique and has different interest's, hobbies, qualities, traits as well as emotional, educational and communicative needs.

Educators need to constantly apprise their students to the fact that they should be inquisitive about seeking information and develop into critical thinkers. Students should be carefully and strategically guided to form their own learning styles and take charge of it. Teachers role is to guide, monitor, evaluate, even allow students to evaluate themselves.

Teachers can appreciate student's abilities, skills and to how they can further enhance their skills. Students need to be aware of their strengths and build upon them.

According to Oxford, learning strategies are specific actions taken by the learner to make learning more easier, faster, enjoyable, more self- directed, effective and transferable to new situation. (1989 P.S)

Metacognitive skills enable students to regulate their thinking, and become independent learners who can enhance their school and life experience whenever the ambitions of our youth lead them they will benefit from being able to solve problems creatively, think analytically communicate effectively and collaborate with others.

Common educational objectives across national and international educational system are reviewed. A balanced emphasis on knowledge and higher order thinking skills. Developing student's metacognitive ability and learning skills is an important learning objective, how to practice self-regulated learning skills at the classroom level. It has been recognized that knowledge skills and understanding are three essential elements of learning and the ties among them set guidelines for curriculum designers (skelton 2002). Important learning abilities and skills (for example critical thinking, creative thinking metacognitive ability) have emerged as important educational goals indicated in the curriculum objectives across different educational system.

For example, creative thinking skills, communication skills, how to provide the proper level of scaffolding in inquiry based learning and to integrate content and skills learning will still require further exploration and metacognitive ability has been emphasized in different content areas at different learning stages in both western and Asian educational system.

Emotional Intelligence in Teaching English:

The teaching job in not only to teach language, but to teach learning affective factors like emotion, attitude, motivation and value influences, learning in an important way. Teachers should empathize will the learners and lower their anxiety by encouraging them and use emotional intelligence while teaching.

Language learning requires motivation and confidence building. All negative emotions need to be suppressed before a student can start learning. Students should be encouraged to stimulate active and healthy emotions, enthusiasm and interest in learning and intellectual development. This positive emotion is a dynamic factor that can influence the quality of teaching and have a fundamental impact. Creating an atmosphere full of positive emotions wherein classroom activities can be easily performed is the purpose of Emotional Intelligence in teaching and learning.

Teenage learners are often quite reluctant to co-operate, after as a result of suppressed fear, anxiety and anger rather than linguistic inability, and are unlikely to learn much in a student – centered classroom. Thus, the teacher needs to focus on areas of language used to express emotions, and on classroom techniques which will reduce tension and produce better group dynamics.

Good language learners control their attitudes and emotions about learning and understand that negative feeling retards learning. Teachers can help generate positive feeling in class by giving students more responsibility, increasing the amount of natural communication, and teaching affective strategies. Techniques like self-reinforcement and positive self-task which help learners gain better control over their emotions, attitudes and motivation related to language

Educators can help students to reflect on their individual learning and engage in metacognitive discussion in class. Educators should celebrate this important skill in large and small group's ways to underscore the many ways this approach comes in handy in the college and other aspects of life, just not students but even their parents can make use of this skill at work. Creating opportunity, releasing potential achieving excellence, Education and skills.

Teachers have a major role in enhancing the self-esteem, emotional growth and motivating students in path breaking learning developing social skills learn work and friendships. Teachers must have knowledge about learning difficulties.

Teachers must lower the anxiety level of students. Brown also state (2007:155) that no successful cognitive or affective activity can be carried out without some degree of self confidence in oneself the belief in one's own capabilities to successfully perform activity. People obtain their sense of self-esteem from past experiences with others and the exterior world. Self-esteem or self-confidence related to language learning experience may be regarded as specific self-esteem which encompasses the acquisition of the language in general and or task self-esteem when considering one particular aspect of the process.

Students and quality instruction should be at the heart of any decision teachers make while building a safe environment for students to learn.

Considering the significance of critical thinking skills in life in general and in formal education in particular teacher should make their best efforts to teach the required skills to their students and the fact that these skills may be unfamiliar, difficult and culturally challenging for students does not justify excluding them from their teaching (Vareghi, Ghelami, Barjestch, 2012).

The revolution in the study of the mind has occurred in the last three or four decades has important implication for education. Teachers can encourage students to relate ideas from a text to their own experiences.

Emotional Intelligence is developed through activities which promote the sharing of ideas and communication in the classroom. Techniques which are already part of the teacher's repertoire of confidence building activities are emphasized:

- A variety of activities maintain interest and allows for different approaches to learning and individual learning styles.

- Ice breakers, warms and mingle activities help students get to know each other and promote interest in lessons if they are related to the topic area.

- Brainstorming and discussion encourages the sharing of knowledge and opinions.

- For some learners, it is easier to reveal themselves Through fictitious role, however, role- plays and simulations should be carefully set up and related to the real world-guided fantasy and drama techniques are useful tools in guiding learners into their roles.

- Group work encourages co-operation. Group composition should be changed often since there is a tendency for high E Q students to work together, but EQ can be also learned by example. Tasks should be designed so that all members have to contribute and have the same outcome- collaborative reading and writing activities as well as group speaking activities may be utilized.

- Project work, students are after Competitive, Group completion of assessed and unassisted projects also encourage Cooperation.

- Giving feedback on performance and making clear what is expected. Feedback should be specific, objective and forced on or aspect of performance the students are able to change.

- Getting feedback on tasks and how students felt during the task

- Continuous assessment allows all positive to be assessed and rewarded including their contribution to the group.

At an institutional level, the emphasis is on creating an environment conducive to raising students Emotional Intelligence. Much of this involves creating a sense of identity, safety and value. In this way, institutions and teachers are responsible for fostering:

- Attachment: A sense of belonging to the college.
- Reassurance: that others experience difficulties.
- Bonding: Facilitating the formation of friendships.
- Induction: Informing students of what is available.
- Training: in study skill, time management and stress reduction.
- Holism: Balancing academic learning with physical and social activities.
- Self-awareness :Recognizing and being able to name our feeling.
- Motivation: the ability to keep going despite failures.
- Self-Regulation: the way we handle our emotion to avoid negative effects.
- Empathy: the ability to read the emotions of others.
- Adeptness: Being sensitive to the feeling of others and handling them appropriately to build positive relationship.

Higher Order Thinking Skill:

Teachers have to constantly encourage students to use higher order thinking by listening and solving problems. It is a challenge for educators to develop their student's ability to ask themselves; as to how they can solve certain problems, analytical thinking, reasoning, logic understanding and thinking beyond the thinking process.

Students should be able to do this at the right time in the right context and respond confidently and effectively by applying adequate cognitive and social strategies.

The most important role of an educator is by constantly modeling questions day in and day out for every lesson so as to get students to become more and more aware of themselves as language learners; what works for them and what doesn't; what their strengths and weaknesses are and what they can do best to address them; how they can effectively tackle specific tasks; what teaching strategies and approaches for pupils with special educational needs; Cognitive or affective obstacles stand in the way of their learning; how they can motivate themselves, how best they can use the environment, the people around them, internet resources etc.., in a way that best suits them.

The role of educators is to identify factors associated with the role of metacognitive learning strategies. Critical thinking is closely associated with metacognitive learning strategies. The aim of higher education should be to facilitate the process of developing a greater ability to anticipate, trigger and take account of change, that is, to become a critical and autonomous person. Students with high levels of critical thinking skills become more independent, self-directed learner because critical thinking enables students to assess their learning styles, strengths and weaknesses and allow them to take ownership of their education (Morgan. N.D)

Innovation in Teaching:

These are small and useful steps teachers can take daily which can help students progress in learning English Language.

At the beginning of each lesson, after stating the learning intentions; what and how they are going to learn. After introducing any task, the educators need to give an example of how they would carry out that task. They can even further take them through the thought process which is called "think aloud". At the end of the task, ask students to self-evaluate with the help of another student, using a checklist of questions.

Educators can further encourage students generate metacognitive questioning by engaging students in group work problem solving activities. From focused to thought processing, the mind shift will enhance students learning.

Teacher's Learning:

Teacher's ultimate goal is to develop inquiring, knowledgeable and caring young people who help to create a better and more peaceful world.

Teachers should further encourage students to become active, compassionate and lifelong learners. Teachers should constantly give feedback to students in order to encourage learners and learning strategies.

Reciprocal teacher – student's conversation. Teachers need to be trained to give feedback in student teacher discussion, various collaborative students to improve self regulated learning. Educators can help students to form short term and long term goals, evaluate and help students to make it achievable by taking practical steps.

Teachers must impart in depth knowledge to students regarding any topic and subject providing many examples of factual knowledge. Teachers must come to teaching with the experience of in depth study of the subject area themselves.

Teachers should use graphic organizers and other visual tools to help make sense of complex information. Teachers can help students by providing them with tools to depict the inter relationship between events or ideas. Graphics organizers are diagram that help students identify main ideas and identify how these ideas are related.

<u>Teacher's Strategy:</u>

Teaching grammar as subject matter can result in language acquisition. Acquisition occurs in their classes when students are interested in the subject matter, "Grammar" when teachers and students are convinced that the study of formal grammar is essential for second language acquisition and the teacher is skilled at presenting explanation in order to make the students understand.

"Once the student has a proper degree of cognitive control over the structure of a language facility will develop automatically with the use of language in meaningful situations "(Carroll, 1966, P-102). In other words learning becomes acquisition.

By monitoring their use of learning strategies, students are better in their track of achieving their goals. Knowing how to orchestrate more than one strategy is an important metacognitive skill. The ability to coordinate, organize and make association among the various strategies available is a major distinction between strong and weak second language learners. Teachers can assist students by making them aware of multiple strategies available to them for e.g. by teaching them how to use both word analysis and context clue to determine the meaning of an unfamiliar word. The teacher also needs to show as to how one strategy is not working and other can.

For e.g. when a student gets to know that word analysis does not work, they can move to other strategies such as context clues to help them understand the word.

The teaching of metacognitive skills is a valuable use of instructional time for a second language teacher. When learners reflect upon their learning strategies, they become prepared to make conscious decisions about what they can do to improve their learning. Strong metacognitive skills empower English language learners.

The role of the teacher is to lecture less and instead direct the students in directions that will allow interactive learning. Teachers must encourage students to find their own way organize information in such a way that they are able to make the most of it. They should be capable of making intelligent guesses. Students should be encouraged to be involved in communication. Voice modulation tone, intonation and learn to vary their language according to the formality of the situation.

Teachers must engage in dialogue, mesmerize them by storytelling, encourage self-introduction. Projects like video making, story writing and skits, should be encouraged.

Evaluation of students can be done on the situational writing, letter writing, Narrative writing, grammar test, vocabulary test, spelling test, comprehension and listening comprehension test, there are many types of methods of assessing students in language learning. It is beneficial to adopt a variety due to different levels of students. Varied learning styles and personalities will affect the performance levels on the different methods of assessing.

Educators must encourage students to interact in second language, like get them involved in role plays, assign projects, encourage independent reading, creative writing assignments, motivate students to volunteer on their own regarding any task. Educators have to have more of hands on activities materials teachers have to give rewards and appreciation as well.

Teachers have to design and plan variety of assignment and have different assessment methods. Teachers have to engage students. To create a word bank from their own reading material, learn to group words into categories. Teachers have to create opportunities for students to ask and investigate questions. They should encourage the students to exhibit personal interest and be a voice in the decision making process. These opportunities are essential for both self regulated learning and motivation.

Teacher can make use of flash cards encourage story telling. In order to enhance students cognitive and metacognitive strategies students can watch videos, movies and discuss about it on line and off line. They should be encouraged to inculcate habits of reading and synthesize exercises. Presentations should be regular feature. Teachers should assess blogs discussion forums Online Chatting, Skype, E-Learning, YouTube videos.

This previous knowledge is the raw material for the new knowledge they will create an important part of the learning process is that students reflect, and talk about their activities. Students also help set their own goals and means of assessment. The teacher helps create situations where the students feel safe questioning and reflecting on their own processes, either privately or in group discussions. The teacher should also create activities that lead the students to reflect on his or her prior knowledge and experience. Depending upon students responses, the teacher encourage abstract as well as concrete, poetic as well as practical, creations of new knowledge.

Teachers have to teach students to construct knowledge through a variety of different venues (cognition) and they identify when they no longer understand and what they can do about it (metacognition).

Students learn more and enjoy learning more when they are actively involved, rather than positive listeners. Education works best when it condensates on thinking and understanding rather than memorization.

Teachers are responsible for setting goals, designing learning tasks and assessing what is learned.

Teachers have to guide students in setting specific goals within the framework of what is being taught, provide options for activities and assignments that capture different students' interest and goals and encourage students to assess what they learn. Teachers have to constantly guide students into higher order thinking skills. Teachers have to encourage students to listen to diverse opinions, have dialogue, engage in critical and creative thinking, and participate in open and meaningful dialogue.

Teachers have to train students in word analysis and word attack techniques. In order to provide students with rich language experiences, including wide ranging discussion's read aloud Conversations on academic topics wide and frequent reading for students.

Teachers should activate existing background knowledge and build new knowledge on it for students.

Learning Autonomy:

The concept of independent autonomy and control in learning experience has gained an increasingly important role in language acquisition.

One of the aims of modern education is training students to become autonomous learner. However unfortunately, as Nunan (2003) puts it, few learners come into any given learning arrangement with the knowledge skills and attitudes that allow them to take part in their own learning. Teachers committed to concepts of autonomy must, therefore, help their learners to develop the relevant knowledge and skills. In addition to setting language content goals, teachers can incorporate a set of learning process goals into their teaching as well.

Students who are capable of analyzing and critiquing ideas can make connections across disciplines and see knowledge as useful and applicable to daily life.

Educators must make learning an enjoyable experience and keep up the burning desire to learn English.

By developing autonomy in students; they become life long, learner's. i.e. they learn how to learn on their own.

The lifelong learning process is defined as "a continuously supportive process which stimulates and empowers individuals to acquire all the knowledge values, skills and understanding they will require throughout their lifetimes and to apply them with confidence, creativity and enjoyment in all roles, circumstances and environments. (Watson, 2003 P.3). Teachers should model thinking skills provide examples of critical ways of thinking. Lesson should be designed in a way to take into account diverse students needs.

Teachers can make use of the information on English language learning strategies and styles to create and design their lesson or course plan. Since, teachers play a pivot role in language teaching, the tools, teaching methods and classroom environment adopted will ultimately affect the student's progress. Teachers have to learn to identify the needs of students according to their requirements and intellectual levels.

Teaching students to drive their brain metacognitive strategies activities and lesson idea.

Teachers have to enlighten the minds of the students that they have the power to unlock their brains amazing power and take control of their learning. Teachers have to constantly have an environment which encourages and motivates students to learn.

Research suggests that metacognition is the key to higher student's achievement, but studies of classroom practice indicate that few students are taught to use metacognition and the supporting cognitive strategies that make learning easier.

Historically, educators focused on the cognitive deficits that students bring to learning tasks which were regarded as relatively fixed and used to explain poor academic performance. By changing our focus to cognitive assets we aim to communicate that strategy for learning performance can be taught, learned and improved with practice.

The cognitive assets make up a tools box of versatile thinking tools that can be taught but not in solution from metacognition.

Metacognition is at the heart of our approach to learning and teaching students to think on a more recent list of 150 factors that influence students achievement, metacognitive strategies were ranked 15th by comparison student social current status (which is after assumed to be a major influence on students learning potential) was ranked 45th (Hathe, 2012). The encouraging conclusion is that the gap between high achievers and struggling students can be closed by guiding the latter to develop a metacognitive approach to learning.

Teaching them how to think about multiple ways to solve problem has helped students become more focused, calm, solve more problems and better at working out things between themselves.

Teachers see knowledge as dynamic, ever changing with their experience. One of the Teachers biggest job is to ask good questions. They have to prompt students to formulate their own question (inquiry). Also allow interpretation and expressions of learning (multiple intelligence). Further person mentoring and group study has to be encouraged as collaboration learning.

Collaborative Learning:

Students are not blank slates upon which knowledge is etched. They come to learning situations with already formulated knowledge, ideas and understanding.

Educators have to help students to make connection, teach students to think, educators have to guide students about the thinking process. They have to think about what they know what connections they can make and what questions they might want answered.

They have to further think about the way the text might be organized such as cause and effect, compare and contrast sequence of events problems and solutions description, narration and so on.

Students on their own do not use metacognitive strategic while reading. For instance, they might just skim through the text without actually understanding it, the content and matter as a whole students study all their subjects for the sake of education but actually they have not been fine tuned to think about are these course content matters.

Therefore, constructing understanding requires both cognitive and metacognitive elements. Role of teachers is to groom students in such a way that they are able to use any strategy at any time and for any purpose. Teaching metacognition imparts within student's life skills for higher order thinking.

Teachers have to explore classroom management techniques and organization which is conductive to learning. It is of imperative importance to consider both the physical and emotional environment that will play a role in the instructional setting. Teacher have to be competent confident and kind. Teachers have to understand the culture background and needs of students. Students need to feel safe, secure welcome and important in the classroom.

Teachers understanding of metacognition and their pedagogical understanding of metacognition and the nature of what it means to teach students to be metacognitive, teaching students to be metacognitive require a complex understanding of both the concept of metacognition and metacognitive thinking strategies.

Learning is enhanced when teachers' pay attention to the knowledge and belief that learners bring to a learning task use this knowledge as a starting point for new instruction and monitor students changing conceptions as instruction proceeds. Teachers' role is to create opportunities for students to learn with understanding. Deep understandings of subject matter transform factual information into useable knowledge.

When students are confused, frustrated or feel left out, the affective filter can prevent them from learning the material. Demonstration and field experiences are other ways to build background knowledge.

Teachers should include hands-on, collaborative inquiry which clarifies concepts and provides opportunities to develop an understanding that transcend linguistic challenges. Rigorous Research Studies on effective instruction for English language learners are unfortunately all too rare.

Teaching students about multiple meanings of the same words (i.e. polygenic terms such a financial institution but can also mean rely on as in "you can bank on him/her). Using visual and graphic organizer will help in conveying meaning. High levels of student's social interaction with each other and with the teachers.

Teacher's role in giving explicit instruction in learning strategies (metacognition) and opportunities to practice using these strategies. These variations can add value and richness to the classroom.

Educators can also help students to activate existing background knowledge by using strategies such as helping students see links between texts and their experiences like text to self-connections, students should also be encouraged to draw from earlier readings or past learning in order to link to new material so as to make text to text connections. While instruction in speaking comes under the umbrella of language arts its application crosses all content across. More among students who have intrinsic motivation for language study and who believe that the study of grammar is essential.

Teachers should develop students self-confidence through regular praise, encouragement and reinforcement making sure that students regularly experience success and a sense of achievement and involving students in more favorable and easier activities promote students self-efficiency with regard to achieving learning goals by teaching students learning and communication strategies as well as strategies for information processing and problem solving, promote favorable self- perceptions of competence in English language by highlighting what students can do, rather than what they cannot do. Encouraging the view that mistakes are part of learning, educators should decrease student's anxiety by creating a supportive and accepting learning environment in the classroom.

Teachers should strive to reduce anxiety activities and techniques; promote motivation enhancing attributes by helping students to recognize the link between effort and outcome and attribute past failure to the use of in appropriate strategies rather than to lack of ability and encourage students to set attainable short term and long term goals.

Appropriate language learning strategies result in greater motivation and confidence. Strategy instructions can enhance learner self- efficacy and autonomous learning and help learners to take responsibility for their own learning. Teachers need to provide learners access to methodological resources and appropriate learning strategies modeling strategies and guidance to help learners make progress and achieve academic success.

Learner's needs and strategies for learning language, should always be at the crux of teaching and learning.

CHAPTER III

CRITICAL THINKING IN ENGLISH LANGUAGE ACQUISITION

CRITICAL THINKING

What is critical thinking?

There is no single definition for Critical Thinking, that is not to say that people struggle to give an explanation of what it means, but simply that they frame it in different ways.

Critical thinking of a passage will help the students to write effective research Papers, Academic writing, Essay writing .By enhancing critical thinking student will learn to create questions that will help them to focus on their reading and writing skills. The student will be able to understand the difference between evaluating and opinion.

Critical Thinking is an approach to language teaching which aims to meet the needs of particular learners. This means in principle that much of the work done by English teachers is concerned with designing appropriate courses for various groups of learners. It seems reasonable enough to assume that a specification of language needs should define the language content of a course designed to meet such needs. Here "learner needs" is open to question. In fact two different interpretations may be extracted from learners' needs. It may refer to terminal behavior, the ends of learning or it may refer to what the learner needs to do to actually acquire the language.

Teaching and curriculum involves not only adhering to the teaching content, but the teaching methodology, learning strategies and the changed relationship between students and teachers. The purpose is to suggest that what is needed for Critical Thinking particularly is a different orientation to English study. There is a shift of the focus of attention from the grammar to the communicative properties and functions of language. Difficulties students encounter arise not so much from a defective knowledge of the system of language but from the unfamiliarity with English use and the adequate rhetoric used to convey scientific facts. It is suggested that in teaching Critical Thinking learning strategies should play not only important but a vital role. Accordingly, autonomous learning and metacognitive strategies are suggested as basics for teaching and learning Critical Thinking and especially in English Language.

English is the accepted international language of technology, science and commerce. English Language has created a new generation of learners who know specifically why they are learning the language. In fact there was a pre-determined goal in their learning English. Whereas English has now became a subject to needs and demands of people other than language teachers. Dovey (2006) states courses which prepare students for the workplace in specific ways can be expected to have purposes quite different from those of discipline- based courses and can also be expected to introduce new questions. Metacognitive Approaches to English Language Acquisition has also become an important part of English, probably as a direct result of the introduction of communicative teaching curricula. Its main drive is practical, driven by the increasing number of people around the world who need English for clearly communicative syllabus design in which he presented a system for devising appropriate syllabus specification from adequate profiles of communicative needs. These profiles included the purposes of communication, the communication settings, and the language skills, functions and structures required.

Critical thinking is defined as an awareness of one's own thinking (self-reflection) and the ability (foundation skills) and willingness (willingness to question) to clarify and improve understanding which aids in drawing appropriate conclusions and making the best decisions possible within a context (knowledge base) (Weissinger, 2003).

Students think that Critical Thinking Skills has been invented by English teachers to make students interested in English programs. They believe that instructors in their field will be more successful for Critical Thinking.

For Students having knowledge in the field is not sufficient for Critical Thinking, they should have a good command in general English and they should be familiar with the basic principles of teaching and learning theory.

Critical thinking is the ability to use self-regulatory mechanisms or cognitive monitoring to ensure the successful completion of the task, such as checking the outcome of any attempt to solve the problem, for example, planning one's strategies for learning, and remediating any difficulties encountered by using compensatory strategies.

Critical Thinking can be about what the person knows and what the person is currently doing. Metacognition is deliberate, planned, intentional, goal directed and future-oriented, mental processing that can be used to accomplish cognitive tasks (Flavell, 1971). Metacognition involves active monitoring and consequent regulation and orchestration of cognitive processes to achieve cognitive goals. As metacognition involves an awareness of oneself as an actor , a deliberate Store and retrieval of information, it may be reasonable to reserve the term metacognitive for conscious and deliberate thoughts that have other thoughts as their objects (Hacker, 1998). According to Block (2004) metacognition can be defined as a reader's awareness of (1) what he or she is thinking about while reading, (2) what thinking processes he or she initiates to overcome literacy challenges, and (3) how a reader selects specific thinking processes to make meaning before, during, and after reading.

To be an efficient and effective thinker, the learner should be able to monitor his or her degree of understanding, be aware of the knowledge possessed, be aware of the task demanded, and know the strategies that facilitate thinking. One example of a specific critical thinking skill is distinguishing fact from opinion. Teaching students to think critically is a difficult task and requires a great deal of patience, decision making and problem solving requires reflective thought and action and it is the ability to use self-regulatory mechanisms.

One approach to teaching critical thinking is the metacognitive approach which emphasizes explaining and modeling the thinking strategy. While reading a student's brain becomes active. After previewing, a student can decide how to deal with any particular text and explore various strategies to have better comprehension. Articles are understood better and students are in a position to skip a few lines to get the gist of the topic.

Reading comprehension can be improved by increasing the speed. Associate knowledge about the topic makes it easier to understand. Finding key words questioning, reasoning, logical reasoning active comprehension are the take-away of critical thinking.

With stiff competition and ever-increasing job requirements, students have to develop their higher order thinking skills such as critical thinking, decision making and problem solving. The current trend of teaching demands that students should be motivated to think and increase their thinking capabilities to be successful.

English literature is one subject in which the thinking skills of a student can be improved. There is a blend of critical thinking skills and subject matter. Thinking skills are reinforced throughout the teaching of the English literature and later retained. Students can enhance critical thinking skills and understanding subject matter simultaneously. A lot depends on the approach used by the educator in the classroom teaching. Students will know what is synthesis of literature and will have different ideas, school of thought, become creative writers and will be able to know the difference between scholarly evaluation and personal opinion.

Critical Thinking Skills

The most effective Critical Thinking Skill seems not to be that which focuses on knowledge at the teachers' own level, but rather that which deals with subject knowledge in terms of how this is taught to students. There is little evidence that the effective teachers of literacy have an extensive command of a range of linguistic terminology. However, it seems likely that having a greater command might help them further improve their teaching.

As with experienced teachers, developing cognitive, metacognitive and affective strategies involves more than simple practical experience. Novice teachers also need to develop an awareness of "why" and "in what" circumstances they might employ particular teaching approaches so as to enhance the application of the above-mentioned strategies. They need not only procedural knowledge about scientific literacy teaching but also conditional knowledge. The development of this knowledge demands the opportunity to compare their experiences with those of others and thus further their proficiency in specific domain knowledge.

Shirkhani & Fahim (2011) believe that language learners who have developed critical thinking skills are capable of doing activities of which other students may not be capable. Whereas earlier the teachers were at the center and the emphasis was put on what to teach, today's education involves teaching how to think, and how learners can be a critical thinker. There is a need to accommodate critical thinking as an essential aspect of teacher education and teacher evaluation programs. According to this research better critical thinkers are better EFL teachers. Ozkan (2010) students who think critically can ask suitable questions, gather relevant information, creatively sort through this information, reason from this information and come to reliable conclusions about the world that enable one to act successfully. These students are more productive while using their second language. Critical thinking skills of English learners help critical thinking activities.

Choy and Cheah (2009) found that critical thinking is encouraged inside the classroom among the students when the teacher provides guidelines for them to use materials related to metacognition effectively. Magno (2010) also obtained the same result as he tested a model where metacognition was used to predict critical thinking. This prediction showed that the ability to monitor one's knowledge and thinking processes helps one to think critically.

This finding supports another investigation by Valeh (2011) who found a significant believes that critical thinking has a vital role in education. He stated that relationship between critical thinking dispositions and metacognitive strategy use. The more metacognitive strategies increase in students, the more critical thinking enhances as well. Making those informed decisions requires critical thinking skills. Therefore, effective participation in public life is contingent on the quality of one's critical thinking skills.

While there is general agreement as to the necessity of developing students' critical thinking skills in preparation for effective citizenship, there is less agreement about how to teach these skills (Wilen in-press). Useful thinking skills include those associated with acquiring, interpreting, organizing, and communicating information; processing data in order to investigate questions; solving problems and making decisions; and interacting with others (NCSS 1993).

Metacognitive Approaches to Critical Thinking:

Critical thinking has a vital role in education. Students who think critically can ask suitable questions, gather relevant information, creatively sort through this information, reason from this information and come to reliable conclusions about the world that enables one to act successfully. In critical thinking a student has to be taught how to analyze or evaluate the 'why' of the statement said.

If a transition and paradigm shift has to be made in teaching and learning in higher education then changes in curriculum design and teaching methods should be considered. Educators must create an environment where a student is encouraged to think, ask questions, reason, analyze debate and come to a conclusion.

The metacognitive approach is an alternative way to teach critical thinking skills and is based on the principles of infusion-the teacher directly teaches students specific critical thinking skills within the context of subject matter. The teacher primarily accomplishes this through modeling the use and application of critical thinking. In addition, the skills are also modeled by the learners.

Cognition or thinking refers to the intellectual functioning of the mind with regard to the learner's ability to attend, acquire, represent, and recall information. Metacognition, which refers to the knowledge and control people have over their own thinking and learning activities (Flavell 1979), deals with the "individual's knowledge about the task, possible strategies that might be applied to the task and the individual's awareness of their own abilities in relation to these strategies" (Taylor 1983, 270).

The teacher shapes students' understanding of the reasoning process by asking them to explain how they made sense of the text. On the basis of what they say, the teacher provides additional explanations to help them reason like experts. Similarly, as they listen to their classmates describing their mental processes, they develop flexibility of thought and an appreciation for the different ways of solving the same problem. Students are asked to pose questions, spot confusions, form hypotheses, and suggest remedies to failures.

A paradigm shift in our education system is required that facilitates development of the critical thinking skills that modern society demands.

Critical thinking opens a space for deeper learning and deeper engagement with the object of learning. Learners employ different thinking skills when learning a language. These can be classified into three types: basic comprehension, critical thinking, and creative thinking. All play a key role in learning and should appear at different points within a lesson, but not necessarily in any order. We believe that up to now the lack of a clear working model—along with a lack of clear examples of critical thinking activities—has prevented teachers from helping learners in acquisition of critical thinking strategies.

Among the several major approaches to teaching critical thinking skills, the literature seems to favor infusion-teaching thinking skills in the context of subject matter. This approach entails integrating content and skills as equally as possible in order to maintain a balance of the two (Willis 1992). Thinking skills are reinforced throughout the teaching of the subject and later retained. Research shows that students learn both skills and subject matter if they are taught concurrently (Beyer 1988).

The metacognitive approach we are proposing is an alternative way to teach critical thinking skills and is based on the principles of infusion- the teacher directly teaches students specific critical thinking skills within the context of subject matter. The teacher primarily accomplishes this through modeling the use and application of critical thinking. In addition, the skills are also modeled by the learners.

There is strong evidence for the effectiveness of the modeling component of the metacognitive approach. One of the most influential studies of critical thinking in social studies classrooms is currently underway at the University of Wisconsin. Newman and his associates are attempting to find out what teachers do to create classroom environments that foster thoughtfulness.

In relation to the acquisition of critical thinking skills, metacognition refers to what a learner knows about his or her thinking processes (conscious awareness) and the ability to control these processes by planning, choosing, and monitoring.

Thinking skills should be encouraged all throughout while teaching English. Critical thinking to refer to the ability to think, analyze, reason and reflect information.

Educators must prepare graduates to evaluate the merit & demerit of proposed solutions. Educators must teach students to perform complex mental operations that will allow them to be successful in their career and personal lines classroom teaching and learning has a deep impact in calculating critical thinking skills.

Thinking processes need to be considered into three broader levels: Basic comprehension, critical thinking, and creative thinking.

Critical thinking can be increased through debates, writing and sharing opinions. Educators and teachers have to create an environment that fosters thoughtfulness. Just nearly explaining the skill is not enough educators have to teach the process and give models to practically apply it in the learning process.

Application of Critical Thinking:

Application of critical thinking in the learning process of learning the English language needs metacognitive approaches in executing the skills.

For example, the teachers can read a text passage during the class and model self-questioning as well as the fix-up strategies adopted to overcome difficulties in understanding. The teachers provide a model of the thinking processes by stating what is going on inside his or her head. Herein the teacher is assumed to be the expert thinkers while the student in seen as the novice.

Students at the multiplicity level realize that uncertainties exist in the world but do not analyze or evaluate why. Students who do not master foundation skills in critical thinking rarely move past the multiplicity position, making this a crucial turning point for development of critical thinking (Kurfiss, 1988; Ryan, 1984). The potential stagnation carries serious implications for higher education. If critical thinking is the desired outcome, but students are only required to memorize facts, evidence is sufficient to speculate that the development of critical thinking skills is not taking place except as a possible result of increase in age or maturity (Chickering, 1981).

A major shortcoming of traditional college classrooms is that faculty presents *products* of their skills, failing to model their own thinking processes for students (Arons, 1985; Davidson & Worsham, 1992; Nelson, 1997). The reality may be that, while faculty value students' upper-level thinking abilities, it is easier to teach and assess lower levels of learning—knowledge and understanding—than to teach and assess higher-order thinking, in particular critical thinking. If classroom activities lie at the bottom of Bloom's (1956) taxonomy of educational objectives, requiring students only to listen passively and recall information, then critical thinking is not consciously being developed, and colleges and universities do not produce the critical thinkers they think they do (Belenky, Clinchy, Goldberger, & Tarule, 1986; Browne & Keeley, 1994; Chickering, 1981; King & Kitchener, 1994).

If critical thinking remains an educational objective, then changes in curriculum design and teaching methods should be considered by Institutions of higher education and faculty in every classroom must provide students with a foundation of critical thinking skills, an environment that encourages the use of critical thinking, and opportunities "to manipulate information and ideas in ways that transform their meaning and implications, such as when students combine facts and ideas in order to synthesize, generalize, explain, hypothesize, or arrive at some conclusion or interpretation" (Newmann & Wehlage, 1993, 9; Facione, Facione, & Giancarlo, 1997).These views need not be exclusive. Foundation skills can and should have Critical thinking.

Auerbach and Paxton (1997), define metacognition as "knowledge of strategies for processing texts, the ability to monitor comprehension, and the ability to adjust strategies as needed" (pp. 240-41). Research studies (Duell, 1986) seem to confirm that as children get older they demonstrate more awareness of their thinking processes. Metacognition is relevant to work on cognitive styles and learning strategies in so far as the individual has some awareness of their thinking or learning processes.

Cognitive strategies differ from metacognitive strategies in that they are likely to be encapsulated within a subject area (e.g., EFL), whereas metacognitive strategies span multiple subject areas (Shraw,1998).Cognitive strategies are, for example, making a decision, translating, summarizing, linking with prior knowledge or experience, applying grammar rules and guessing meaning from texts (e.g., O'Malley and Chamot, 1990). Metacognition refers to awareness and control of cognitive activities. Empirical studies show that successful learners differ from less successful ones in both the quantity and quality of cognitive and metacognitive strategy use (e.g., Oxford, 1989). The literature of metacognitive strategies in reading comprehension reveals that poor readers in general lack effective metacognitive strategies and have little awareness on how to approach to reading. They also have deficiencies in the use of metacognitive strategies to monitor for their understanding of texts In contrast successful English Language readers know how to use appropriate strategies to enhance text comprehension (e.g., Pitts, 1983).

Similar to experiences about metacognitive strategies with intermediate-level students in Critical Thinking courses worldwide.

Application of Critical Thinking enables Students to think more actively in reading as if, students read with their brain rather than their eyes. After previewing Students can decide how they will deal with any particular text, and which other strategies they are going to follow to have better comprehension.

Critical strategies help Students to be more conscious and active. They are used to read a text word for word until then, being afraid to misunderstand the contents. Critical Thinking helps Students to skip as many words as possible even when they are going to read about something not familiar, and are going to deal with the text in which they already have knowledge. Students are able to co –relate and understand the contents of articles. Reading speed can be predicting by the following contents. Students can associate their knowledge concerning the topics and which can help to make their learning much easier. Finding key words in any text is an interesting technique. Relying on Key words is more helpful than relying on the structure in reading a text.

It is easier to ask questions when students read something. To have prior knowledge with because they have something to base-in to ask questions. Students have critical reading and they can use their background knowledge.

Infusion-Teaching Thinking Skills:

Among the several major approaches to teaching critical thinking skills, the literature seems to favor infusion-teaching thinking skills in the context of subject matter. This approach entails integrating content and skills as equally as possible in order to maintain a balance of the two (Willis 1992). Thinking skills are reinforced throughout the teaching of the subject and later retained. Research shows that students learn both skills and subject matter if they are taught concurrently (Beyer 1988).

In relation to the acquisition of critical thinking skills, metacognition refers to what a learner knows about his or her thinking processes (conscious awareness) and the ability to control these processes by planning, choosing, and monitoring. Basically, there are two components of the metacognitive process: awareness and action.

The teacher decides which skill is to be taught, lists the steps to follow when executing the skill, and explains why it is important and when students will need to use it. One example of a specific critical thinking skill is distinguishing fact from opinion. For example, in teaching learners to distinguish fact from opinion, the teacher begins by defining the skill.

English language has traditionally been a staple discipline in general education. However, in a college English language instruction has not consistently integrated critical thinking in its approach to teaching and learning. Explicit teaching of critical-thinking skills in English language courses would strengthen higher-order thinking skills while enhancing language and cultural proficiency.

Today in our ever-changing and challenging world, students are required to go beyond the scope of their knowledge. They need to develop their higher-order thinking skills, such as critical thinking, decision making, and problem solving (Profetto-McGrath, 2003; Riddell, 2007; Sezer, 2008).Ku (2009) States, "besides the ability to engage in cognitive skills, a critical thinker must also have a strong intention to recognize the importance of good thinking and have the initiative to seek better judgment".

Marin and Halpern (2011) explicit and imbedded instructional modes were compared and critical thinking was assessed with Halpern Critical Thinking Assessment, which uses constructed response and multiple-choice response formats with everyday situations.

Thinking skills are reinforced throughout the teaching of the subject and later retained. Research shows that students learn both skills and subject matter if they are taught concurrently (Beyer 1988).

Accepting critical thinking as an educational ideal brings with it ramifications for *what* we teach and *how* we teach. A paradigm shift in our education system is required that facilitates development of the critical thinking skills that modern society demands.

Development of thinking skills is not a natural occurrence, an accidental outcome of experience, or an automatic by product of study in a subject area (de Sanchez, 1995; Taba, 1965, as cited in Beyer, 1987). It requires deliberate, continuing instruction and practice in order to develop it to its full potential (Arons, 1979; Kirby &Goodpaster, 1999; Perkins, 1985, as cited in Beyer, 1987; Thoms, 1998). Unfortunately, the traditional instruction paradigm, a 50-minute lecture intended to disseminate information, cannot fulfill critical thinking objectives (Barr &Tagg, 1995), and critical thinking will not take place if a student's goal is simply "an exit score from school necessary to enter a professional course, [which only] involves surface approaches to learning with Critical Thinking.

Critical thinking, which involves knowledge of strategies as well as a propensity toward applying them, is a major component of higher education and a national priority for American colleges and universities(Brookfield, 1987; National Education Goals Panel, 1991; Nelson, 1994; U.S. Congress, 1994). The broadly defined benefits of higher education are often operationalized under the construct of critical thinking (Wood, 1997); in other words, the aim of higher education is to transfer abstract principles to concrete applications. University mission statements contain references to critical thinking, but have colleges and universities cultivated student awareness of difficult real-world problems and prepared their graduates to evaluate the merits and demerits of proposed solutions? While faculty in all disciplines want students to perform complex mental operations that will allow them to be successful in coursework, in future careers, and in their personal lives (Pellegrino, 1995; Siegel, 1980; Weiss, 1992/1993), is higher education doing its job? The answers to these questions have concrete implications for what happens in the classroom and how it is assessed.

Critical Thinking in English Language Teaching is sensitive to what is fair and balanced. Robert H. Ennis's (March, 1992) often cited definition describes critical thinking as "reasonable reflective thinking focused on deciding what to believe or do." The British philosopher Bertrand Russell (April, 1959) said that when studying any matter, we must ask ourselves "what are the facts, and what is the truth that the facts bear out. Never let yourself be diverted, either by what you wish to believe, or what you think could have beneficent social effects if it were believed; but look only and surely at what are the facts." Few would argue with these sentiments. However, in reality we may not always be able to make judgments based solely on facts, since often those facts are incomplete or unavailable to us at a given time. In these instances, the critical thinker must either reserve judgment or try to arrive at a conclusion that is reasonable, in other words, a conclusion that is as free from bias and prejudice as is possible. To sum up, in our working model, we would like learners to view critical thinking as a mindset that involves thinking reflectively (being curious), rationally (thinking analytically), and reasonably (coming to sensible conclusions). Critical thinking skills are not just a box of tools to be used when needed and then put away but derive from a mindset that involves seeking knowledge in a particular way. A critical thinker's skills are in continual use, not just as an exercise, but as part of a considered and holistic approach to learning (National Council for Excellence in Critical Thinking, 1987). Just one note of caution here: This mindset, which Dewey (1910) called a "healthy skepticism," does not mean a subversive or cynical approach. Rather, it simply means a curious and considered one. The idea is not to challenge ideas aggressively, but to seek to understand how these ideas were arrived at. We would like learners to view critical thinking as a mindset that involves thinking reflectively, rationally and reasonably. We believe that teachers should stimulate and nurture this mindset by integrating critical thinking activities into their lessons. A good way to explore to what extent your students already possess a critical mindset is to do an activity. It can raise learners' awareness of critical thinking in general or can be used to promote critical thinking in students as they prepare for a debate or write an opinion essay.

Use of Critical Thinking In English For Specific Purposes (ESP):

In recent trends English for specific purposes (ESP) is in sync with Critical Thinking which proposes that all language teaching programs should be tailored to the specific learning and language needs of students

Today English is a widely accepted International Language of Technology, Science, and Commerce. Students have a great need to learn the English language. In fact there is a pre-determined goal in their learning English language. English has now become a subject to needs, and demands of people other than language teachers.

Dovey (2006) states courses which prepare students for the workplace in specific ways can be expected to have purposes quite different from those of discipline-based courses and can also be expected to introduce new questions. ESP along with Critical Thinking became an important part of English as second language teaching in the 1970s and 1980s, probably as a direct result of the introduction of communicative teaching curricula. Its main drive was practical, driven by the increasing numbers of people around the world who needed English for clearly defined reasons such as reading academic textbooks or transacting business (Hutchinson and Waters, 1987). It is suggested that ESP could easily be outlined based on the sorts of texts that learners need to become familiar with, or the needs-related nature of the teaching (Swales, 1985). The early analyses of ESP texts took the form of frequency counts of structures or verbforms, but such analyses only provided descriptions and had little or no explanatory force.

These limitations, together with the increasing importance of the communicative aspects of the language and an increasing interest in linguistic use rather than form, led to researchers using rhetorical or discourse analysis methods to discover the main characteristics of texts in different academic fields (e.g. Widdowson, 1979). During the late 1970s ESP course designers started to carry out a needs analysis of their students' future linguistic requirements. These needs analyses were often expressed in terms of notions and functions (Wilkins, 1976) and the most celebrated model of such needs analysis are described by Munby (1978) in his communicative syllabus design in which he presented a system for devising appropriate syllabus specification from adequate profiles of communicative needs. These profiles included the purposes of communication, the communication settings, and the language skills, functions and structures required.

The Practical Problem

An ESP teacher lives with the question whether an English teacher or the specialists from the field should teach an ESP. Some students think that ESP is a new label for English for General Purpose (EGP) and nothing else. For them this is invented by English teachers to make students interested in English programs. They believe that their instructors in their field will be more successful to ESP courses even not being familiar with English teaching and learning theories. For some others having knowledge in the field is not sufficient for an ESP Instructor, they should have a good command in general English and they should be familiar with the basic principles and teaching and learning theories.

Suggested Solution to the Problem:

To make things clear it is better to have a brief look at some definitions and explanations by some specialists in the field to support the idea that ESP is not the same as EGP. One of the generally accepted definitions refers to Hutchinson and Waters. What is the difference between the ESP and General English (EGP) approach? Hutchinson and Waters 1987:53) answer this quite simply, "... in theory nothing, in practice a great deal". This definition by Hutchinson and Waters raises one important question. If in theory there is no difference between ESP and EGP, what is the theoretical justification like Metacognition is cognition about cognition or thinking about doing. Metacognition is deliberate, planned, intentional, goal directed and future-oriented mental processing that can be used to accomplish cognitive tasks (Flavell, 1971). Metacognition involves active monitoring and consequent regulation and orchestration of cognitive processes to achieve cognitive goals. As metacognition involves an awareness of oneself as an actor, a deliberate Store and retrieval of information, it may be reasonable to reserve the term metacognitive for conscious and deliberate thoughts that have other thoughts as their objects (Hacker, 1998). According to Block (2004) metacognition can be defined as a reader's awareness of (1) what he or she is thinking about while reading, (2) what thinking processes he or she initiates to overcome literacy challenges, and (3) how a reader selects specific thinking processes to make meaning before, during, and after reading.

Application of English for specific purposes and Critical Thinking enables students to:

1. Think with their brain and be more active in reading.
2. Students will be able to preview their text and can decide how to deal with any particular text, and which other strategies they are going to follow to have better comprehension.
3. Students can skip as many words as possible while reading about something not familiar with, and then deal with the text, of which they already have knowledge.
4. Thinking about the topics will help students to understand the contents of articles.
5. Students will be able to associate their knowledge to the concerned topics and help make their learning much easier.

6. Finding key words will be interesting technique and helpful.
7. Students will find it easier to frame questions with prior knowledge English for specific purpose and Critical Thinking is an approach

to English language teaching, which aims to meet the needs of English Language learners. This means in principle that much of the work done by ESP teachers is concerned with designing appropriate courses for various groups of learners. It seems reasonable enough to assume that a specification of language needs should define the language content of a course designed to meet such needs. Here "learner needs" is open to question. In fact two different interpretations may be extracted from learners' needs. It may refer to terminal behavior, the ends of learning or it may refer to what the learner needs to do to actually acquire the language.

Higher Order Thinking Skills Versus Lower OrderThinking Skills:

In order to understand how critical thinking occurs within a language learning exercise or lesson and so arrive at a working model, we need to see it in the context of other thinking skills involved in learning. In other words, as well as describing activities that demand critical thinking, we need to describe activities that draw on other cognitive processes. For this, we start with the work of Benjamin Bloom and others who have created taxonomies for thinking. In particular, we need to consider the notion of higher-order and lower-order thinking skills, since these are commonly used reference points for framing educational curricula. It is important to stress from the outset that higher-order thinking does not imply superior thinking skills and lower order inferior ones. Each is an important element of learning in its own way. Bloom's taxonomy in his 1956 work - A Taxonomy of Educational Objectives, Handbook 1: Cognitive Domain, Bloom investigated how different types of thinking lead to learning. His work sought to build a classification of learner behaviors "in the cognitive domain." Bloom's taxonomy was cumulative: that is to say, each behavior or mental process was built upon the preceding one, starting with the simplest and ending with the most complex. First came knowledge, without which you could not have comprehension, then followed application, analysis, comprehension, and very little time was spent on analysis, synthesis, and evaluation—"the higher mental processes that would enable students to apply their knowledge creatively" (Bloom, 1994, p. 1). While Bloom (1956) himself never used the term "critical thinking"—instead, he referred to "intellectual Critical Thinking in English Language Teaching (ELT)Bloom's work stimulated an interest in how educators could more explicitly incorporate higher-order thinking skills in their programs. In 2001, Bloom's colleague David Krathwohl and student Lorin Anderson revised the taxonomy by classifying the thinking skills as shown in Figure

1.2. In their schemes the different thinking skills were described using verbs rather than nouns, and were no longer seen as cumulative and hierarchical. Even though the six cognitive levels are still arranged in order from lower to higher as in Bloom's original taxonomy, Krathwohl and Anderson preferred to see these different skills as being of equal value, and employed at various times in learning. Educators using Krathwohl and Anderson's taxonomy of thinking skills Cognitive Processes like Remember, Understand, Apply, Analyze and Evaluate could more explicitly incorporate higher-order thinking skills in their programs.

Remembering involves students recognizing and recalling what has been taught. This could be tested, for example, by having students match a list of eight words to their definitions. Alternately, in a reading lesson, remembering could be tested by having students answer Who, What, and When questions, that is, questions that elicit a recall of key words and facts. Understanding involves students constructing meaning by connecting new knowledge with existing knowledge. For example, in the English Language Teaching (ELT) classroom a teacher could show students the rule for forming regular verbs in the simple past tense. As a result, students understand that when they see a verb ending in "ed", it indicates a past action. Because they already know the base form of various verbs and the present tense, they are now able to distinguish between past and present actions in reading or listening exercises. Applying involves students testing out this newly gained knowledge, usually in a controlled way. Examples of applying include having students take a phrase and Analyzing involves students breaking concepts down into individual parts and seeing how they contribute to overall structure or meaning. At this point we move into so-called higher-order thinking— what Anderson and Krathwohl (2001) call—"an extension of Understanding" and a "prelude to Evaluating or Creating" (p. 79). Examples of analyzing include reading an argument and identifying supporting evidence or connecting questions with conclusions. Analyzing can take place at text level, as in the above examples, or it can take place at the word or sentence level, for instance, when students try to work out a grammatical rule from language in context. Evaluating involves students making judgments based on their own or someone else's criteria.

Evaluating naturally flows from analyzing. It is in these two levels of higher-order thinking that we see classroom activities that are typically described as critical thinking tasks, especially in the receptive skills of reading and listening.

Examples of such tasks include having students analyze a text to identify the different arguments, and then evaluate which are the most and least convincing; or having students solve a problem collaboratively by discussing the merits of different solutions, and then selecting the best plan of action to follow. Evaluating also includes checking and critiquing others' work, for example, watching peers give a presentation and then giving feedback.

The first three types of thinking (remembering, applying and understanding) are what have come to be known as lower-order thinking and the latter three (analyzing, evaluating and creating) as higher-order thinking. Central to Anderson and Kratwohl's revised taxonomy was the idea that the different types of thinking are part of a continuum in which the levels overlap and flow back and forth from one to the other (Krathwohl, 2002). In this way, teachers initiate tasks that practice different thinking skills at different times, and sometimes more than once, in no Critical Thinking in English Language Teaching It is worth noting here that although many people equate critical thinking with the skills of analyzing and evaluating, Anderson and Krathwohl themselves make no such assertion. Rather, they say that classroom activities that could be described as critical thinking "most likely call for cognitive processes in several categories; ... critical thinking and problem-solving tends to cut across the rows" (Krathwohl, 2002, p. 267). A working model for critical thinking in English Language Teaching "The six thinking processes" characterized by Anderson and Krathwohl seem, at first, apt descriptions of activities that take place in the language learning classroom. However, if we adhere too closely to the six levels as a way of framing critical thinking in English Language Teaching, we very soon run into trouble. Questions are raised that are difficult to answer: is understands really a lower-order thinking skill? Aren't the skills of analyzing and evaluating part of understanding? What is the difference between applying knowledge and creating? These are gray areas. Accordingly, our own framework classifies the thinking processes that need to be considered into three broader levels: basic comprehension, critical thinking, and creative thinking. The levels overlap, with the weight given to each in a typical lesson reflected in the space it occupies in the diagram. Much of what is traditionally done in learning in language teaching is at the level of basic comprehension, and often less time is devoted to critical thinking and creative thinking.

Basic Comprehension Example:

Basic comprehension means understanding the essential meaning of a word, sentence, text, or idea. In many cases—for example, reading a cooking recipe, learning the meaning of a concrete noun (e.g., warehouse), or interpreting a sentence such as "I leave the house at 6:30 AM in the morning to drive to work"—basic comprehension will suffice. There is little to be gained from further reflection or analysis. Teachers devote a great deal of classroom time in helping students comprehend language and ideas at this basic level: matching words or phrases to pictures, answering true or false questions about a reading text, discussing what sports people like to play, and so on. By basic comprehension, we mean understanding the essential meaning of a word, sentence, text, or idea. Included in the idea of basic comprehension is testing learners' ability to recall and then apply language in a controlled way to show that they have learned it. This could be something as simple as completing a sentence with a missing word: The products are stored in a large for distribution around the world.(answer: warehouse). Alternately, it could be a more demanding activity, such .This lower-order thinking, which we can broadly refer to as basic comprehension, will seem familiar to most teachers around the world. It links in with a historical model of teaching where students are presented with new language, then practice it in a controlled way, and finally try to produce it in a more open (or personalized) context to demonstrate they have "learned" it.

Skills and Abilities Associated with Critical Thinking:

Following are some of the skills and abilities associated with Critical Thinking:

- Inquisitiveness and intellectual curiosity
- Objectivity and truth-seeking
- Flexibility
- Open-mindedness
- Self-evaluation and self-regulation
- Intellectual skepticism
- Perception and interpretation of information
- Systematic analysis and inference
- Persistence

- Decisiveness

Teaching learners to think critically is a difficult task and requires a great deal of patience. But the time and effort are well spent in trying to prepare students capable of making decisions, and solving problems using reflective thought to guide action for the common good. One approach to teaching critical thinking is the metacognitive approach, which emphasizes explaining and modeling the thinking strategy. The metacognitive approach proposed serves as a guide for teachers interested in orienting their teaching towards helping learners become more analytical and independent thinkers.

While there is general agreement as to the necessity of developing students' critical thinking skills in preparation for effective citizenship, there is less agreement about how to teach these skills (Wilen in-press). Useful thinking skills include those associated with acquiring, interpreting, organizing, and communicating information; processing data in order to investigate questions; solving problems and making decisions; and interacting with others (NCSS 1993).

There is strong evidence for the effectiveness of the modeling component of the metacognitive approach. One of the most influential studies of critical thinking.

Based on the research conducted to date, primary dimensions of classroom thoughtfulness have been identified. These are observable qualities of classroom activity and talk that facilitate students‘ development of subject matter understanding, thinking skills, and dispositions of thoughtfulness. The most important characteristic is the demonstration by the teacher of how he/she has thought through problems, rather than the mere provision of answers. This is modeling. Other characteristics are that the teacher shows interest in students' ideas and their approaches to solving problems, and acknowledges the difficulties students have in understanding problematic topics (Newman 1991).

The teacher is the "expert" and models the thought processes involved in executing a particular critical thinking skill, such as establishing whether a statement is fact or opinion. The teacher breaks this skill down into steps and demonstrates the execution of each step by thinking aloud.

According to Sanacore (1984), metacognition is "knowing what you know," "knowing what you need to know," and "knowing the utility of active intervention." However, this metacognitive skill is apparently not developed in all students. To be an efficient and effective thinker, the learner should be able to monitor his or her degree of understanding, be aware of the knowledge possessed, be conscious of the task demanded, and know the strategies that facilitate thinking.

The teacher decides which skill is to be taught, lists the steps to follow when executing the skill, and explains why it is important and when students will need to use it. One example of a specific critical thinking skill is distinguishing fact from opinion. For example, in teaching learners to distinguish fact from opinion, the teacher begins by defining the skill. The ability to think critically is considered an important component of a college education, and secondary institutions typically include critical thinking in student learning outcomes, particularly in the general education curriculum.

Metacognitive reading strategy awareness plays a significant role in reading comprehension and educational process.

Metacognitive reading strategy skill plays a key role in reading comprehension education success. Students have to be honed with Metacognitive reading strategy skills. Metacognitive reading strategy and comprehension needs more focus in current trends of English language Teaching and learning.

There is a close relationship between metacognitive reading comprehension and metacognitive reading strategy skills Metacognitive reading strategy ability needs to be focused in language learning and teaching.

Metacognitive reading comprehension skill has a positive effect on learning a second language the skills they need for effective communication in English.

With top trends and demands of international communication travelling and studying abroad students need to learn four skills of listening, speaking, reading and writing for their success.

But reading comprehension is the most important skill for English language learning, students mainly struggle in construction meaning and understanding of the texts. Metacognitive reading strategy can faster reading comprehension among students.

Many students of English Language learning have major difficulties with English reading comprehension ever after years of learning the English Language. This often results in them facing difficulties in areas such as finding employment or a better job.

Readers who use Metacognitive reading strategy in their reading comprehension are more successful than other readers who do not utilize this strategy in reading comprehension process.

Questioning, visualizing and synthesizing information are all ways that readers can examine their thinking process. By practicing and applying Metacognitive strategies.

Students will become good readers, capable of handling any text across a curriculum Metacognitive strategies enable students to develop a deeper understanding of a book's theme or topic.

They learn to construct knowledge through a variety of methods and choose the right tools to correct the problem students need to take their thinking process to a higher level and express themselves clearly. Good readers plan before reading. Students think about the text topic, read the title, author, table of contents, study illustrations, graphics and captions.

Students further think about the cause and effect compare and contrast, sequence of events problem and solution, description and a combination of these texts.

Students who take responsibility for their own comprehension constantly question the text and their reactions to it.

Other ways that students can enhance their Reading and comprehension are by making connections, predictions, inferences, context clues by using graphic organizers to pinpoint types of text information write self-stick notes in the margins, questions of comments.

When good reader's finish reading, they reflect on the strategies they used to determine whether their plan worked or not or should they do something new. If after-re-reading through the text students are able to answer the questions, students may determine that they understand the material. Thus, the metacognitive strategy of self-questioning is used to ensure Critical Thinking in understanding & Comprehension.

Listening Comprehension, a basic skill is a challenge for English Language Acquisition.

This challenge arising may lead to frustration, poor listeners performance or inadequate attention paid in the classroom. The complexity of listening may involve external factors related to speaker, text, or content. These factors new expressions, speech rate, accent, unfamiliar content and cultural references, increase the difficulty of listening.

To reduce the complexity for less skilled listeners, "metacognitive instruction" is used to develop and facilitate the process of listening comprehension. The metacognitive used in a listening lesson should feature authentic and natural everyday speech. The listening lessons using the strategy-based approach help listeners enlarge their working memory capacity to embrace more language chunks for future recall. Teachers should identify less-skilled listeners listening development and keep encouraging the listeners to reflect on their listening.

The educators encouragement assists the listeners to build up with listening bricks to form a good listening comprehension ability listening is the basic and essential language skill that needs to be instructed like other skills.

Speaking is considered as an important language skill it is given less importance in English teaching classrooms teachers usually focus on writing, reading and grammar and they neglect speaking.

English Language learners are required to use what they learn in the classroom to hone their speaking skills outside students have to motivate to take charge of their own speaking skills. It has been observed that students struggle to speak fluently despite its importance in career.

Teachers need to promote only when teachers are metacognitively aware will they make use of efficient strategies at class to motivate students in the ability to write competently is closely connected to the ability to read a variety of texts students can write response before after reading.

Writing strategies help students learn content in a more useful way when these strategies help students activate prior knowledge and help them set their own purposes for reading.

When students are given group assignments, students work together in pair's or small groups to discuss their ideas before writing these collaborative discussions influence English Language learners writing skills writing is a strategy which should be taught and utilized across the content areas. Teachers are expected to play roles as guide, facilitator, and assessor, partner, communicator, source of information and organizer.

English writing class can be student-centered by ways means of essay appreciation. Teachers guide students get inspiration, motivation from each other students focus on the problems in writing share ideas and cooperate to find answers to the problems. Eventually, through practice they begin to adopt the new method of Education.

Students eyes have to be opened up to all that writing Skills could be in English . English language writing is frequently accepted as being the most challenging Language skill to be acquired. Only a few students are able to write spontaneously, when as some students feel comfortable writing a formal task. Most of the students find it difficult to express their ideas leading teachers finding an effective strategy on improving student writing.

Teachers on their part have limitations of course design teaching purpose, limitations of course design teaching, purpose, limited time and mostly teaching methods.

Students can however be encouraged into active writing, class including group discussion, debate, brain storming, asking questions, model composition, flash fiction, story-telling, paragraphs, Narratives of different scenario's, personal Experiences to bring out the best from them with poetry being a great-channel of Expression.

In English teaching and learning speaking is considered a skill to be practiced and mastered.

The speaking skill is viewed as the most important part of English language learning. The growing need for international communication in the information age has led many language learner's to improve their speaking ability, student's who are effective communicators experience more success in their careers knowledge of grammar, vocabulary, pronunciation and intonation is not adequate but the ability to use this knowledge in order to communicate successfully is indispensable.

We use words not just to express our thoughts but also to shape them Developing Critical thinking skills is thus essential to understand the ways in which words can be useful to express our thoughts.

Educators have to foremost hone their metacognitive and creative thinking skills effectively and only then will they be able to transfer their knowledge and skills to their students.

The integration of Reading, Writing, Speaking & listening skills in learning English Language.

It is recommended that further research be conducted to determine the best way to group students for collaboration when incorporating reading, writing, speaking and listening tasks within content area instruction.

- Speaking

    - Talking Box Activity
    - Collaborative group Discussion.
    - Choose a corner Argument Activity
    - Group sharing of writing.

- Writing

    - Analysis Tool organizers
    - Essay- organizer
    - T-Chart
    - Essay

- Reading

    - Background information
    - Explanations of images
    - Documents
    - Descriptions

- Listening

    - Collaborative group Discussions
    - Choose a corner Argument Activity
    - Viewing Evaluating film clips
    - Group sharing of writing.

There is a shift of the focus of attention from the grammar to the communicative properties and functions of English language. Use of course have to be such the students include critical thinking which prepares them for their workplace. This is different from discipline based courses and can also be expected to introduce new questions driven by the increasing number of people around the world who need English for transacting business.

CHAPTER IV

METACOGNITIVE STRATEGIES IN ENGLISH LANGUAGE ACQUISITION

METACOGNITIVE STRATEGIES

Strategy Definition:

Successful learners are active, goal-directed, self-regulated and assume responsibility for their own learning. In other words, it is important to help the student be aware of their own learning process, starting with a goal in mind and using it to plan as to how to achieve, monitor and evaluate the learning objectives.

Strategy can be defined as:

1. Previewing the main idea
2. Concepts of a text identifying the organizing principle.
3. Planning how to accomplish the learning task
4. Planning the sequence of ideas to express.
5. Attending to keywords, phrases, ideas, linguistic types of information
6. Self-Management Plan - when – where - how to study.
7. Seeking or arranging the conditions that help one learn

Monitoring:

Monitoring is checking one's oral or written production while it is taking place.

Monitoring involves:

1. Monitoring Think while listening
2. Monitoring Comprehension Think while reading
3. Checking one's Comprehension During listening or reading.
4. Monitoring Production Think while speaking / writing

Evaluating:

Evaluating is self-assessment by keeping a learning log and reflecting on what you learned and judging how well you have accomplished a learning task.

Self- Assessment:

1. 1. Check book
2. 2. Keep a learning log
3. 3. Reflect on what you learned.

Cognitive Strategies:

1. Resourcing Use reference materials
2. Grouping Classify Construct graphic organizers
3. Note making Take notes on maps, To do lists

METACOGNITIVE STRATEGIES

Metacognitive strategy is application of active learning that emphasis on student reflecting on the learning process to achieve the objectives.

Metacognitive knowledge and experience appear to play key roles in every human endeavor. More accurate one's metacognitive knowledge, the greater the success in learning.

Metacognition is popularly known as "thinking about thinking" or "cognition about cognition". It refers to a person's knowledge about their own learning and thinking process (Flavell, 1979). Such knowledge is used to monitor and regulate cognitive processes during learning and thinking activities in the context of learning awareness of the processes used, plays an important role in the development of student learning skills.

The use of a metacognitive approach is recommended by educational psychologists to provide opportunities for students to learn about their learning process, thereby helping them to acquire the intended knowledge and skills.

The Metacognitive skill is thinking about those techniques that one can apply to remember the words. Beyond the technique one's mind can think of developing further techniques to make memorizing easier.

One of the challenges facing university is that of equipping graduates with the capacity for independent analytical thinking so as to operate in a global context. The ability to think analytically and to learn independently calls for learners to be purposeful, strategic and persistent in learning. This is the role of metacognition in learning autonomy across domains.

Metacognitive process includes planning, mentoring, problem solving evaluation, among other things. Metacognitive strategies help build something more than an inclination towards cooperation namely self-esteem and self-confidence given by the ability to choose and evaluate one's learning strategies, besides the value of the respective strategies the autonomy and independence in learning that comes along with them.

Existing metacognitive expertise refers to the understandings of declarative, procedural and conditional knowledge, about the world, a person's cognitive and affective states and activities, duties and strategies that are saved in one's lengthy term memory. Thought tactics at the cognitive stage contain the expertise and techniques required to reap the cognitive desires such as tackling a task or two a problem. Affective states and things to do with emotions, attitudes and the beliefs a individual holds and how they reply to situations. Metacognitive notion procedures are those directed at strategy acquisition and governing the knowledge and strategies represented in lengthy time period memory and in cognitive concept as nicely as in the external situation, in this case the task/problem. They include monitoring, evaluating, problem-solving and planning processes.

The executive controller is the voice of a person's mind. It functions as a retriever of statistics to which monitoring or evaluating tactics correspond and as a commander of these processes. That is, records gained will be selected, in contrast and combined, or discarded. The command for similarly records can be completed in the place necessary. Consequently, this mental gadget makes remaining decisions about the expertise and strategies to whole a task, to supply it up, to resolve a problem, or what to be discarded and what to be saved in long-term reminiscence or to alter what is known. The executive controller tells one whether the venture is too challenging or easy. It tells one how to deal with a undertaking or a problem. It commands one to put in greater effort or to supply up. Furthermore, it makes choices and orders other processes. The activation or inactivation of the executive controller indicates to what extent metacognitive engagement occurs.

Language Learning Strategies:

Learning strategies are used by the learner to help one to acquire or to take input (rewrite) and use the information to make ones learning quick, simple, more effective which can be passed on to new situations, a learner wants to learn English language to communicate in English fluently and correctly. Language autonomy can be acquired with the help of learning strategies. Managing is a must for autonomy; self efficiency also can be improved by learning strategies.

There are six major learning strategies: Cognitive, Mnemonic, Metacognitive, Compensatory, Affective and Social.

1. **Cognitive:** - learners already have information, they add this information with new information, analyzing, questioning, inductive and deductive reasoning, rearranging the information and taking regular notes of the information are examples of cognitive strategies.
2. **Mnemonic**: - mnemonic strategy assists learners to connect a newly learned knowledge with what they have already learned and know.

1. **Metacognitive Strategy**: -They assist learners to manage themselves as learners. Each learning style approach helps to learn a language. Learners can select the learning style which suits him best. Metacognitive strategy helps as learners to select the right resources and fix a goal for language learning. If the goals are not clear the learning process will have obstacles.
2. **Compensatory Strategies**: - Guessing the meaning or idea while listening and readying fills a learning gap.
3. **Affective Strategies**: - Positive attitudes improve language learning.
4. **Social Strategies**: Social strategies are integral part of communicative language learning.

A thrust hold level of proficiency in cognitive English language learning is essential for the learner's participation and engagement that is necessary for subsequent success in learning English Language. Ways to develop this form should be learned in authentic concept rather than through contrived drills in language work books.

Think aloud, thinking skills, small groups, enable participants to hear. From the student's everyday lives and using it as a spring board to interest them in academic concepts. Research shows that when students are interested in something and can connect it to their lives or cultural backgrounds, they are more highly motivated and learn at a better rate.

Metacognitive strategies called self-directed learning skills in literature and regulatory skills in the cognitive English Language Learning, refer to executive processes that govern and direct other thought processes when planning monitoring, evaluating, regular solution activity.

Most teachers are familiar with the term metacognition, would describe it as thinking about thinking when we use metacognitive strategies, we anticipate or plan for a task, consider the success of the implementation, and evaluate the success of the plan afterwards. Metacognitive process includes planning, monitoring, problem solving, evaluating, among other things.

This study highlights the aspect that Educators need to place enough importance on many metacognitive strategies especially ones which might help poor students in English (e.g. planning and problem- solving strategies). Learners have to be strongly motivated to learn, show students how to overcome obstacles give them the confidence and ability to cope with study. The motivation to study independently and Creation of autonomous learning environment.

The role of metacognitive strategies is promoting learning. Metacognitive knowledge experience in using strategies encourages learner's motivation and ability to learn independently. These way learners take charge of their own learning.

These positive learning experiences will help them see difficulties. Obstacles, weaknesses or failure as challenges which can be overcome by the application of appropriate strategies.

The absence of higher-level metacognitive processes, lessons and learners willingness, ability to take charge of his/her English learning, is to some extent in line. That is learning is more effective when learners are actively involved in the learning process, assessing responsibility for their learning and participating in the decisions which affect it.

Some strategies such as using hints, body language, rehearing, re- reading responding in class are obviously listening or reading specific while other i.e. preparing for class, preparing to confront obstacles might be affected by language proficiency.

Metacognitive strategies play an important role for success in learning across disciplines as well as being closely linked to the development of independent learning. Many contributions to research suggest that metacognition is common to learning both content and language learning.

Insight into the metacognitive strategies that students from different disciplines possess and the interaction of the strategies when learning content knowledge and language is an initial step to promising language learning autonomy understanding of learners existing knowledge and experience learning about learner independence (in learning the major subject disciplines) can provide teacher/ instructor with clear. Explicit guidelines on how learners can develop their independence in language learning consequently learners will be enriched with adequate learning strategies to develop a love of learning.

In this strategy learners consider the task at hand and look at the text or materials they will be using by doing a "book-walk" or other previewing activities. Students see how the text will help them answer specific questions, how it relates to the topic at hand and so on. Just as a meaningful objective helps students to know what to look for in advance organization can help them to understand how the materials relate to the task at hand and help them plan for their learning.

Selective Attention: Students can do selective reading and gather information for their task. Teaching students to look for just the information needed for the task at hand helps them build efficiency and avoid confusion in a short span of time.

Monitor Comprehension: Good reader and listener monitor their comprehension and take action. Comprehension breaks down while reading, listening, speaking and writing. Students can monitor their own comprehension when producing language feedback.

Language learning strategies: Metacognitive Development providing students with skills and vocabulary to talk about their learning e.g.: - self assessments, note taking, study technique and vocabulary assignment establishing a link between the student's prior knowledge to the material and familiarizing concepts through direct experience.

Text Representation: Inviting students to extend their understanding of the text and apply them in a new way, students can create drawings, video, and invent games.

METACOGNITIVE STRATEGIES IN ENGLISH LANGUAGE LEARNING

Six key strategies for teachers of English language learners:

The following six key strategies help students develop English as a second language and also learn words that are not part of everyday English:

1. Vocabulary and language development Teachers have to introduce new concepts by discussing vocabulary words, key to that concept and build students background knowledge
2. Guided interaction: Teachers structure lessons so that students work together to understand what they read – by listening, speaking, reading and writing collaboration about the academic conception of the text.
3. Metacognition and authentic assessment rather than having students simply memorize information teachers' model and explicitly teach

thinking skills (Metacognition) crucial to learning new concepts for learning English language and a skill used by highly proficient readers of any language.

4. The fourth strategy is explicit instruction or direct teaching of concepts academic language and reading comprehension strategies needed to complete classroom tasks.
5. The fifth strategy is the use of meaning-based context. Universal themes, referring to taking something meaningful from the students everyday lives and using it as a spring board to interest them in academic concepts, research shows that when students are interested in something they can connect it to their lives or cultural background they are more highly motivated and learn at a better rate.
6. The final strategies in the use of modeling graphic organizer and visuals. The use of a variety of visual aids including pictures diagram and charts helps all students and especially English language learners' students. They easily recognize essential information and its relationship to supporting ideas. Visual aids make both the language and the content more accessible to students

The purpose of learning strategies is to give students the tools they need to be independent, effective, efficient and strategic learners.

There are further few more strategies that Teachers can use while teaching English.

<u>1. Planning Goal Setting</u>

Planning Goal Setting includes:

- Pre-reviewing concepts
- Expecting the encountered problem
- Predicting outcomes/ answers
- Predicting the incoming information
- Choosing strategies for the task work.

<u>2. Monitoring</u>

Monitoring is checking one's comprehension during listening or reading. Monitoring includes:

- Checking progress
- Seeking related prior knowledge

- Checking the retrieval of required information.
- Note–taking
- Selectively checking appropriateness of the strategy
- Checking correctness of the predictions/answer
- Checking the linkage to other subjects
- Checking importance of the information
- Self-examination.

3. Problem Solving.

Problem Solving includes:

- Revising the plan
- Accessing various resources
- Tolerating incomprehension
- Managing resources linking with prior knowledge
- Inferencing
- Elaboration

4. Evaluating

Evaluating includes:

- Judging that the goal has been met
- Assessing strategy used within subject
- Applicability
- Seeking other suitable strategy
- Assessing knowledge/ information comparing new with known knowledge
- Judging how much learned
- Summarizing ideas/ lessons
- Assessing learning / work.
- Judging worthiness of learning
- refining ideas/ skills
- Applying learning to other practice.

Metacognitive strategies comprise of few major categories which arementioned below:

Direct Strategies are creating mental images, sounds and reviewing employed actions.

Indirect Strategies: - Metacognitive Strategies that involve centering your learning arranging, planning and evaluating your learning.

Cognitive strategies: - Practicing receiving and sending messages analyzing and reasoning creating structure for input and output.

Affective strategies use positive attitudes that improve language learning. Such methods lower anxiety level encourage students to do more and take control of their emotional temperature.

It includes:

1. Lowering your anxiety
2. Encouraging yourself
3. Taking your emotional temperature.

Compensation Strategies: - Guessing intelligently, overcoming limitations in speaking and writing.

Social Strategies: Social strategies are integral part of communicative language learning.

They include:

1. Asking questions
2. Co- operating with others
3. Empathizing with other

Students must be strongly motivated to learn the above strategies to overcome obstacles. It is the responsibility of the teacher to help build the confidence of the students and their abilities to cope with the studies. The motivation to study independently and creation of autonomous learning environment has to be created by teachers.

Metacognitive knowledge experience in using strategies encourages earner's motivation and ability to learn independently. These way learners take charge of their own learning. This positive learning experience will help them see difficult obstacles, weaknesses or failure as challenges which can be overcome by the application of appropriate strategies.

Learning is more effective when learners are actively involved in the learning process, assessing responsibility for their learning, and participating in the decisions which affect it. Some strategies such as using hints/ body language, rehearsing, re-reading, responding in class are obviously listening or reading specific, while other i.e. preparing for class, preparing to confront obstacles might be affected by language proficiency.

2. Strategy Development using Reference Materials:

The following reference materials can be used for Strategy Development:

1. Dictionaries, encyclopedias or textbooks.
2. Classify words, technology, quantities or concepts according to their attributes.
3. Writing down key words in abbreviated verbal, graphic or numerical form.
4. Elaboration of prior knowledge.
5. Use what you know, use background knowledge, make analogies.
6. Relating new to known information, making personal associations

3. Strategies for using Computers for Teaching English Language:

In addition to printed materials, teachers, can bring in computer aided audio-visual equipment into the language classroom and build games and activities round them in order to stimulate language learning. These include objects from the real words, referred to as 'regalia' and also pictures, flash cards and wall charts. Almost every sample of language from real life, like newspapers, advertisements, instructions on the use of consumer products, billboards, etc. can be used as a language teaching resource.

In this age of information technology, there is hardly any sphere of human activities that has not been impacted by Computers and have added a new dimension to educational technology. Technology cannot replace the teacher in the classroom, but can lend assistance to facilitate learning, as a classroom aid.

The computer aided audio and video sessions provide inputs which could lead on to dialogues and discussions. The activities and learning that take place are independent of the computer program itself. Computers can be used for teaching some aspect of Language. Software programs as well as interactive CD ROMs are available, where lessons are programmed, graded and sequenced so as to facilitate self-learning. These materials can be accessed directly by the learners who can select the area of learning and adjust their pace of learning.

Computer lessons can address all the four skill areas – listening, speaking, reading and writing. It also makes distance learning possible as well as conventional. Many universities have begun offering courses through e-mail or CD ROMs.

To sum up the advantages of computers in language teaching:

1. Computers can control presentation. It can combine visual and graphic information with text. It can highlight features using colour and movement.
2. Computers can provide novel and creative stimuli for learning. New language can be learned in an interactive mode.
3. Computers provide immediate feedback and this can be used for error correction. It can also help in error-analysis.
4. Computers adaptability helps teachers to adapt instructional materials to suit the needs of the students.

4. Writing Strategies:

Students need to develop polished writing skills for a number of reasons. Writing makes one's thinking and reasoning visible which is an important skill in academic setting and many workplaces. Instruction in writing is often not explicit instead many teachers expect students to automatically transfer what they know from reading into writing. This is problematic for all students as proficiency in reading does not guarantee proficiency in writing.

Writing strategies includes teaching students strategies for planning, revising and editing. Students should be encouraged to plan, draft, revise and edit their compositions. Teachers should assign students specific reachable goals. Educators should encourage students to construct more complex sophisticated sentences.

However, other things that have to be included in language learning are:

- Study skills
- Self-assessment
- Working with other people
- Using resources
- Memory learning styles
- Motivation
- Emotions
- Self-belief
- Managing learning and so on.....

For eg., when reading narrative texts, educators can ask students to imagine the story like they are mentally playing a movie and can benefit information retention and deep understanding.

Most of the early investigations of metacognition were descriptive in nature in that they sought to describe general developmental pattern of children's knowledge about memory processes. They were particularly interested in processes concerned with conscious and deliberate storage.

5. Planning Strategies:

Planning a strategy involves:

1. Setting own objectives keeping them in mind.
2. Identifying in advance the aspect of information to look for and focusing on that particulars information.
3. Deciding what is already known about the subject topic or issue that will be helpful. Thinking in advance about strategies and tactics that one can use to understand the subject topic or issue.
4. Trying to find out what can be done in sequence, to make lectures or texts understandable, checking periodically whether the material is making sense.
5. Using various kinds of resources to make understanding clear e.g. graphs charts, key concepts, reference material outlines.

6. Goal Setting Strategy in English Language Learning:

By preparation and planning in relation to their learning goals students think about what their goals are and how they will go about accomplishing them. Students with the help of the teacher can set a realistic goal within a set time for accomplishing that goal. Setting clear challenging and realistic goals can help students see their own progress and hopefully by becoming consciously aware of their progress the students' motivation for learning would be increased.

Students have more chances of good success when they set goals for learning strategies. Students should be explicitly taught that once they have selected and begun to use the specific strategies they need to check periodically whether or not those strategies are effective and being used as intended. For example while reading they can use context to guess the meaning of some unknown vocabulary items to monitor them they should pause and check to see if the meaning they guessed makes sense in the text. If not, then they should go back and modify or change their strategy.

Knowing how to use a combination of strategies is an important metacognitive skill. Research has shown that successful language learners tend to select strategies that work well together in a highly orchestrated way tailored to the requirements of the language task. These learners can easily explain the strategies they use and why they employ them.

The metacognitive ability to select and use particular strategies in a given context for a specific purpose means that the learner can think and make conscious decision about the learning process. Learners should be taught not only about learning strategies but also about when to use them. The goal of the students should be how to choose the most appropriate strategy in a given situation.

Other things that need to be included in our model of the strategies of language learning are study skills, self-assessment, using my first language working with other people using resources, using memory learning styles, motivation, emotions, self-belief, managing learning.

Repetition: What makes something stick in memory is repetition. Anything that the student learns must be contextualized, broken into chunks of information using mnemonics and only then will the student be able to memorize it.

Power of Questioning: Questions must be asked as much needed to find out if the student has properly understood the text.

Brainstorming: This is also a good strategy to have a mind map and to focus on a few things only and take things bit by bit.

Cognitive and metacognitive strategies can be made interesting by giving choice strategies which give them solutions to current learning problems. All strategies have to be short, interesting and visibly useful in the minds of students.

This suggests the need to give explicit training to students in all the four metacognitive processes and further a need for training in metacognitive strategies to promote autonomy in English learning.

The final strategy is the use of modeling graphic organizers, making use of a variety of visual aids including pictures, diagrams, charts, visuals, etc., make both the language students understand, the content more accurate according to vocabulary and language development .

1. Teachers introduce new concepts by discussing vocabulary words; key to that concept builds students background knowledge.

2. Guided Interaction: - Teachers structure lessons so students work together to understand what they read by listening, speaking, reading and writing collaboratively.

3. Metacognition: Metacognition and authentic assessment, teachers learn thinking skills (metacognition) crucial to learning new concepts. Research shows that metacognition is a critical skill for learning a second language and a skill used by highly proficient readers of any language.

4. Explicit instruction or direct teaching of concepts, academic language, reading comprehension.

5. Meaning based context and universal themes referring to taking something meaningful.

Finally, Metacognitive Strategy is application of active learning that emphasis on students reflecting on the learning process to achieve the objectives. Successful learners are active, goal-directed, self-regulated and assume responsibility for their own learning process, starting with a goal in mind and using it to plan as to how to achieve, monitor and evaluate the learning objectives. Ultimately Teachers tailor instruction to meet the needs of diverse group of learners. Together, Teachers and Students, develop their understanding of each other, the world around them and the Language that connects them all.

Conclusion

Finally, it is necessary to consider acquisition. At first, the meaning of acquisition may also seem self-evident, but on further reflection are compounded by the use of terms such as learning and development to refer to similar construct. In many cases the terms acquisition and learning have been synonymous, but some researchers particularly Stephen Krashen (1982, 2003) in the acquisition learning hypothesis of his Monitor Model of SLA, have made significant distinctions between the two terms, with learning referring to the accumulation of metalinguistic, declarative knowledge about the English language and acquisition referring to gaining the implicit English Language, knowledge that results in learners' ability to use the English Language for communication. These processes and types of knowledge are important to distinguish, in keeping with current English Language usage, the terms learning and acquisition will not be used in to convey these distinctions instead, terms such as implicit and explicit knowledge or declarative and procedural knowledge. Will be used while learning and acquisition will be used interchangeably. Another term that is sometimes used to refer to acquisition is development. There are slightly different connotations between acquisition and development with the former emphasizing the end product of learning while the latter underscores the process of learning. Yet in both cases, there is the notion of an increase in English Language proficiency and it is this idea that will serve as a general definition of acquisition.

It's time that Teachers switch with Globalization its imperative that teachers adapt themselves to a new paradigm shift of teaching learning methods curriculum, and application of learning theories. Teachers have to equip themselves with new methods and strategies. We have to use English for social, professional and academic purposes.

English Language Acquisition has contributed a wealth of research on how knowledge of the first and English language universally influences acquisition.

It is noteworthy that internal cognition is assumed to be the focus of learning (hence the word 'cognitive' in the term) and that a clear separation between cognitive-internal and social-external worlds is presupposed, since how the two interact is the object of inquiry.

Languages are almost always learned with others, and these others generate linguistic evidence, rich or poor, abundant or scarce, that surround learners. Knowing about English language benefits is important for achieving a good understanding of how people learn English language.

Much in the linguistic environment, particularly in naturalistic settings, but also in today's communicative classrooms, comes to learners in the midst of oral interactionwith one or more interlocutors, rather than as exposure to monologic spoken or written discourse. Learning happens through comprehension and that more one comprehends, the more one learns. The more learners notice, the more they learn, and that domains of human learning, plays a minimal role in the challenging business of learning English language.

There is direct connection between Interaction and English language Acquisition. Ehrlich et al. (1989) found that not all people who happen to have grown up with a language are equally skillful at using it to deliver the kinds of explanations required from the tasks that researchers use in cognitive-interactions studies.

Motivation is perhaps the most important question that teachers and learners of English language ask themselves: How central is motivation in explaining the relative degree of success that different people encounter when they attempt to learn English language? That is, how much can motivation buy us in predicting successful English Language learning?

Many current psychologist favor the cognitive functional approach to language which emphasizes that we structure our language so that listeners will pay attention to the information we want to emphasize.

Neurolinguistics research shows that the left hemisphere typically performs most language processing but the right hemisphere interprets a message's emotional tone decodes metaphors and resolve ambiguities.

English language has four impressively complicated cognitive tasks. Speech comprehension, reading, speaking and writing. These tasks require the simultaneous coordination of cognitive skills and social knowledge. We can marvel that human beings can manage all these tasks in one language. But then we must remind ourselves that many people master two or more languages.

Metacognitive Approaches to English Language Acquisition is a new research area supplemented by, and challenged by, a newly developing model one with its roots in the fields of neuroscience and artificial intelligence. The living brain with its myriad neurons and interconnections appears to process information during the acts of perceiving, recognizing, reading, and problem solving. Some of the basic concepts of the neural network approach of mind and thinking have brought to the field of English Language Learning ,along with higher order cognitive processes and skills. Metacognition is concerned with the nature of language and is followed, in turn, by one that emphasizes the comprehension of speech and the written word .Strategies entertain the topic of problem-solving, that of decision making and reasoning; address the utilization of knowledge in laboratory and real world contexts and the nature of the skills required therein.

Studies relating language to brain functioning are examined, Writers in the popular literature have talked about using the left and right halves of our brains to accomplish a myriad of cognitive activities including language acquisition.

The right hemisphere specializes in language because It is evident, that certain areas of the left hemisphere play an important role in language capability for humans.

Long agreed with Krashan that learning happens through comprehension and that the more one comprehends the more one learns, swain proposed that producing the target language may be the trigger that forces the learner to pay attention to the means of expression needed in order to successfully convey his or her own intended meaning (P-249). If learners push themselves to express their intended meaning more precisely or if the nature of what they care with words (i.e. the task) in demanding cognitively and linguistically when most researchers could envision a casual role in English Language learning only for comprehension. Optimal English Language learning must include opportunities for language use that is slightly beyond what the learner currently can handle in speaking or writing and production which is meaningful and whose demands exceed the learners current abilities is the kind of language use most likely to destabilize internal interlanguage representations. By encouraging risk full attempts by the learner to handle complex content beyond current competence, such conditions of language use may drive learning.

Cognitive resources such as attention and memory are limited. Two types of memory are crucial, in all cognitive operation, long term memory and working memory both are fundamentally involved in English Language processing and learning.

Together with memory attention is another essential component of cognition. One main characteristics of attention is that its capacity is limited. Only one attention demanding processing task can be handled at the same time.

English language is related to success in work and studies and thus English Language as knowledge is perceived to have pragmatic consequences. English language has been given special status as a world language that evokes positive as well as negative symbolic image of globalization economic process.

Metacognitive- having clear goals for improving one's own skills, noticing one's own mistake, cognitive, guessing from context writing notes, memory related (C.g. Connecting word sound with a mental image or picture).

Cognitive or learning styles are ways in which individuals prefer to put this general cognitive ability to use.

Learning strategies are conscious mental and behavioral procedures that people engage in with the aim to gain control over their learning process. Strategies can be cognitive (among which memory related and compensatory strategies are important) metacognitive social and affective) English language learning and social learning are Outcomes for reaching and includes normative ways of viewing the world. That is by increasingly participating more actively in activities with other learners acquires new ways of saying doing and being.

English Language Acquisition is about succeeding in attaining material , symbolic and affective returns that they desire for themselves and it is also about being considered by others as worthy social beings. In both cases, learners are engaged in changing their worlds and thus English Language Acquisition is always transformative. Students need to be proficient in reading, writing, speaking, and listening for them to be job-ready. Teachers need to promote students learning initiatives by using autonomy and Metacognitive Strategies. Overall Students Greatly benefit from Metacognitive

Approaches to English Language Acquisition which raises their awareness and builds confidence in them. The overall aim of this study is to instill and pave way for students. To achieve mastery over English Language Acquisition and be successful in their career. It is hopeful that this Research inspires new thoughts and makes contribution in the study of Metacognitive Approaches in English Language Acquisition.

Critical Thinking is a significant predictor of achievement. Students come to the University and College lacking in Critical Thinking and

Metacognitive Skills and abilities because of the Educational System in India which is heavily dominated by the Standardized Tests.

There is a need for generating a stronger emphasis on Metacognition in Language Teaching and Teachers to become more interested in developing their own and their learners Metacognition.

Based on the findings obtained from the present study, teacher's critical thinking and metacognitive beliefs require questioning. Educational strategies need a change and should incorporate critical thinking and metacognitive strategies instead of simple lecture format teachers need to hone metacognitive strategies and inculcate Critical Thinking strategies and Metacognitive skills in listening, writing, reading & speaking. It is also recommended that teacher education program redesign their Curricula based on research observation presentation and other types of activities. Teachers should provide students an environment in which metacognitive strategies approaches and critical thinking skills are valued rather than giving students a multiple choice test or open-ended exams.

Students should be encouraged to think Critically from the earliest years of their education. Metacognition is a set of skill that enable learners to become aware of how they learn and to evaluate and adopt these skill to become increasingly effective at learning in a world that demands lifelong learning providing people with new and improved metacognitive strategies is a gift that can last forever students can also enhance their own English language learning by developing their own metacognitive processing strategies.

Experienced educators know the structure of English language,, teaching learning with cognitive road maps to guide the students the assessments they use to gauge student progress and the questions they ask in the give and take of classroom life flowing with the current trends in the field of learning English language tools of technology. Job requirements different curricula have emerged along with needs for new pedagogical approaches that are more student centered all with the objectives of promoting effective learning.

At a time when the importance of English language Acquisition to individual fulfillment and economic success has focused attention on the need to better equip our students for academic achievement by investing in high quality education system of teaching and learning.

Inclusion of Metacognitive approaches in teaching and learning enables students to have autonomy in the learning process, they get involved in group activity, form their own strategies to hone their English proficiency skills and even have an understanding of problem based learning, students are exposed to hands on activities, Audio-visual second language materials, materials that are in-depth and have real-life applications in different contexts scenarios have an understanding of logical reasoning, constructive criticisms students will have a positive rapport with their teachers, friends and acquaintances, introduction of rewards and appreciation will foster further motivation for learning among students. Holistic Development of students can have a cutting edge with inclusion of human values.

Above and beyond learning English language should be a pleasure and an enjoyable experience for students.

Language teachers have to be aware of students personality as a factor in order to optimize their students learning English language, teachers have the autonomy to use various learning styles and strategies more, which is also well encouraged and celebrated.

A good amalgamation of all these strategies and tools should be on its way to achieving effective language learning and effective language teaching a goal we all want. Educators must keep up the burning desire to learn the English language to excel in the competitive world.

This book is bound to provide food for thought and a valuable source of inspiration not only for academics wishing to obtain fresh insights into crucial attributes but also for teacher educators intent on fostering metacognition in prospective teachers and educators willing to become more reflective in their own teaching and to enhance the awareness of language and language learning in their students.

9 798887 045641

Printed by Libri Plureos GmbH in Hamburg,
Germany